Advanced Praise for

Digging Up the Truth and Other Big Bay Stories

"Faye Bowers' stories, collected here, are a delightful, sometimes sad, but always entertaining, compilation of histories about those who lived, loved, and died in the small village of Big Bay, Michigan. What's so compelling about these tales from the shores of Lake Superior is how Bowers' journalistic focus so vividly revitalizes them. It is as if we were there. Whether it's spooky seances, whimsical class trips, or tragic drownings, the joys and heartaches of the folks in these stories come to life in Bowers' capable hands. Bowers' prose gift is in the care she takes in telling these ordinary citizens' very special stories."

— Randy Tessier, English professor at University of Michigan who summers in Big Bay

"This is a magnificent work of journalism and love by Faye Bowers, my amazing editor and friend. It is a work of love for family, community, and Big Bay, Michigan, her hometown. Reading it will make you long for your hometown and inspire you to search for your roots as well."

— David Rohde, author, investigative journalist, and executive editor for news at *The New Yorker* website

"You probably have some great family stories, and if you haven't asked your grandparents about them yet, don't waste any more time. But it's highly unlikely that your family stories will be quite as spellbinding as Faye Bowers' *Digging Up the Truth.* Yes, Faye's family stories from the Michigan north woods include bologna salad, salty grandmothers, and berry-picking expeditions—all delightfully told. But they also include everything from a nun throwing a crucifix to a headless skeleton under the apple tree. Don't miss it."

— Ann Hilton Fisher, who loves the UP,
good writing, and local history

"Faye and I worked for the same newspaper in Boston. We each chose to leave that crowded, self-centered city to move to rural areas—I chose Vermont; Faye chose the Upper Peninsula of Michigan. We both appreciate the people in these areas for the character and values they hold. Her people live in Big Bay for some of the same reasons Vermonters live where they do. The winters are long, and the reasons to live there are subtle and sometimes hard to see. But they *choose* to live there. Faye's stories about the people from Big Bay are wonderfully realized and her details show her characters' humor and their occasional sadness as well. Read on."

— Jeff Danziger, syndicated cartoonist

"They say Lake Superior doesn't give up its dead, but Faye Bowers gives up Big Bay's past in these six tales to ensure family members and local legends are not forgotten. A fine mix of storytelling and documented facts, *Digging Up the Truth and Other Big Bay Stories* celebrates a remote area full of real-life 'characters' whose hard work, big dreams, and idiosyncrasies bring twentieth-century small town America back to life."

— Tyler R. Tichelaar, PhD
and award-winning author of *Haunted Marquette*
and *Kawbawgam: The Chief, The Legend, The Man*

Digging Up the Truth
and
Other Big Bay Stories

Faye Bowers

Dedication

For my mother, Dorothy French Bowers, and her siblings: Peter Raymen French, Vernice French Temple, and Mildred French Fleury. They loved Big Bay and grand adventures. They instilled that love in me. And in memory of my oldest brother, Claude, right in the photo, and for my older brother, Bert, for his invaluable memory.

Contents

Introduction

Late July 2002—My sister Linda and I sat on the front porch of Pete TenEyck's cabin, sipping coffee as we stared out at ever-changing Lake Superior. The sun had been shining brightly, but dark, ominous clouds began to roll in our direction over Black Rock Point.

We had thoroughly enjoyed our annual vacation—at the cabin we rented each summer for more than twenty-five years—in our hometown of Big Bay. The remote, tiny town in the Upper Peninsula of Michigan was carved out of the thick forests by lumber barons some 125 years earlier. Up to that time, it was pristine, undeveloped—inhabited only by nomadic Ojibwa and a bounty of wild animals.

Fortunately for us, it never became highly populated. After the booming lumber business cycled through and headed farther west, the town pretty much remained the same size—about 300 people give or take a few. It is located about twenty-five miles northwest of Marquette between a large bay on Lake Superior and an inland lake, Independence. It is literally at the end of the road, an oasis of enchantment and tranquility, far removed from life in the big cities where my sister and I now lived.

This was the moment we'd been anticipating—and dreading. The first cloudy day, we had agreed, we'd set out on our yearly trek to the

Birch cemetery, where our forever-young uncle and aunt—victims of a 1920s typhoid outbreak—were buried. Grandma French started the tradition. Every spring of my childhood, we'd drive down to the Yellow Dog Swamp to dig up trilliums to plant on those two little graves in the overgrown, unmarked cemetery at Birch.

This would be the first year we'd travel to the remote location on our own because our lifelong guides and curators of family stories, our mother, Uncle Raymen, and Aunt Vernice, were no longer with us. They now lay at rest a short drive up the road in the Big Bay cemetery, along with so many others from our family.

With the mantle now firmly in our hands, and fortified by good, strong coffee, Linda and I drove down the Big Bay Road toward Marquette. But somehow, the turnoff that leads to Saux Head Lake and Loma Farms looked different than it had just a couple of years before, and the two-track logging road that led up the hill to the cemetery had become overgrown. We searched and searched but couldn't find it. We called our older brother, Bert, who lives in Marquette, to help. He showed up and led us to the graves, next to a giant pine, which was our north star for locating the spot.

The loss of our family members, who had led us there so many times and passed down numerous stories of what life had been like in Big Bay in "the old days," hit us hard. We'd lost them in a short time. It not only left us as the first line of defense against immortality, but without elders we could ask about the days of yore.

That made us extremely sad and sorry we had not been as interested as we could have been as young people, when we could have asked so many more questions. But it eventually provoked me to interview as many old-timers who remained as possible and to begin collecting photographs, newspaper clippings, court documents—anything I could to keep the stories we heard alive.

That, in turn, led to this collection of short stories. Some are about family members; others are about people who lived, thrived, and died in Big Bay. Besides Big Bay, they have one other thing in common: They were all ordinary people. But they either accomplished extraordinary things or had extraordinary things happen to them. And they matter. They matter to me—and to Big Bay.

You see, even though Big Bay is at the end of the road and feels as if it will always be small and unscathed, it isn't. The people here are subject to the same dreams, schemes, ups and downs, as well as world and national challenges as people anywhere.

1. Take the title story, "Digging Up the Truth." I began to write this story solely about the 1939 drowning death of Uncle Dockie (Murdock Bowers), which occurred ten years before I was born. But as I began to draw on my memories of what I was told about the drowning, as well as those of my siblings and other relatives, I realized my story couldn't possibly be complete without bringing in other members of the family, especially larger-than-life Aunt Belle.

2. Then there is "In the Beginning: The LeClaire and Burns Families." The history of Big Bay is inextricably linked with these intermarried families. They inhabited this area long before Powell Township was incorporated in 1904, and many descendants live here to this day. This was the most difficult story to report and write because I could find no one with living memories of the elder members of these families. But I've cobbled together as complete a story as possible with the help of written records and a family member who has extensively researched the LeClaire and Burns family trees.

3. Next, there's Rose Anna Lucy in "Old Lady Lucy and Her Twenty-Five Cent Moonshine." The scariest woman in Big Bay, she ran a speakeasy during Prohibition and found herself

on the wrong side of the law. Her punishment: three years in the first women's penitentiary in the United States.

4. After that, there's "The Civilian Conservation Corps Arrives in Big Bay." Like the rest of the country, Big Bay was hit hard by the Depression that followed the 1929 stock market crash. One of the US government's responses was the creation of the Civilian Conservation Corps, a program that put young men to work to help support their families and at the same time preserve and protect the country's national resources. The boys benefited; so did Big Bay.

5. And then, "From Big Bay to Detroit: 1947 Class Trip." I wrote this piece on a whim. I met Kitty (Katharine Spehar L'Huillier), a classmate of my older brother, Bert, by happenstance one day. She shared with me some of her memories of my older siblings, especially Bert, and their 1947 class trip—the first trip Powell Township School graduates made that left the Upper Peninsula. A version I wrote of this story first appeared in the Winter 2018 issue of *The Chronicle*, a publication of The Historical Society of Michigan.

6. Finally, there's Great-Uncle Pete in "Big Bay, Beyond, and Back." The romantic notion of the Wild West and the prospect of financial security lured him in 1923 to drive a Model T Ford from Big Bay to Seattle, where he boarded a ferry for Alaska. He spent nearly a year there and purchased several blue foxes, which he brought back to Big Bay to start his fox farm. On the trip out, his route took him a little farther north than necessary, but he wanted to attend a World Heavyweight Boxing Championship on July 4, 1923, at Shelby, Montana. A version I wrote of this story first appeared in the Spring 2015 issue of *The Chronicle*.

In some cases, the stories aren't as complete as I'd like them to be. But I've taken them as far as I am able. Maybe someday, someone else can build on them. I sincerely hope you enjoy them and appreciate Big Bay and those who have lived here as much as I do.

Digging Up the Truth

Aunt Belle sits across from Dad at our kitchen table, the one with the yellow marbled Formica top and chrome legs. She speaks in a hushed, hoarse whisper because she's not sure I'm asleep.

I'm not. I lie wide-eyed with anticipation in my bed that's pushed tight against the thin wallboard separating me from the kitchen. The narrow doorway at the end of my bed is covered with a thin, faded burgundy curtain, which makes it easy for me to eavesdrop.

Aunt Belle is notorious in our family for telling suspenseful, scary stories. Plus, she pretty much runs the show—everyone's show.

But the account she begins to unravel chills me more than the late fall breeze gusting through the bedroom window. It is yet one more attempt to get to the bottom of the 1939 disappearance of their younger brother, Dockie.

She explains to my dad that she is now convinced Dockie didn't drown in Lake Superior after all, or even row his boat over to Canada. Now, she says, she is sure their younger brother was the victim of a murder and cover-up.

"I took Sister Theresa from St. Michael's Church down to the beach," Aunt Belle, a recent convert to Catholicism, whispers.

"Sister Theresa stood with her back to the lake and threw her rosary over her shoulder."

I immediately form a picture in my head. I see this large penguin-like figure waddling on the shore of Lake Superior. Next to her is stout and gray-haired Aunt Belle, clad in a cotton print housedress, covered by an ever-present pinafore apron, and scampering to keep up in her black, chunky heeled, sturdy shoes.

But wait a minute. Didn't she just tell my dad the week before that she was able to pull in a Canadian radio station on her big RCA Victor, and that she was sure she heard Dockie singing one of his favorite tunes over the air waves? She told my dad she believed it was Dockie's way of letting her know he was alive and well in Canada. It was proof he lived up to his word. Aunt Belle said Dockie confided in her about his unhappy marriage and swore he would one day escape from it by jumping in his boat and heading across the lake for Thunder Bay.

Still, I was riveted to this latest explanation by Aunt Belle's new expert on life and death, Sister Theresa. Aunt Belle said Sister explained how the rosary toss worked as they drove the thirty miles from Marquette to the Burns compound in Big Bay, a piece of beautiful sand beach on a large bay of Lake Superior for which the town is named.

Sister Theresa would stand on the old Burns property with her back to the lake and toss her blessed rosary over her left shoulder. If the cross anchored to the middle of the rosary pointed toward the lake when it landed, it would mean Dockie's remains were somewhere in the depths. But if the cross pointed away from the lake, that would mean Dockie was still on land.

Sister Theresa's cross alighted in the sand, pointing away from the lake and directly at the small, two-story square log cabin where Dockie had lived with his part-Native American wife and four children. Dockie's wife, Aggie Burns, was the granddaughter of Morris LeClaire, a member of the Ojibwa tribe who built the original structure and was known as the first permanent inhabitant of that land.

Aunt Belle was now convinced that Dockie's wife, or others on his behalf, killed him and buried him in the cellar of that house. She pleaded with Dad to drive to Big Bay with her to dig up that cellar. I gasped and almost tumbled out of bed to beg my dad to stay out of it. But I buried myself under the covers instead because I couldn't let them know I was listening.

This latest supposition of Aunt Belle's surfaced in the fall of 1960 and was the latest of her efforts to get to the bottom of what truly happened when Dockie disappeared, allegedly drowned in Lake Superior, known locally as The Big Lake.

The story of Dockie's disappearance—like so many handed down over a couple of generations—has more than one version and has evolved. The official one—as reported by the October 24, 1939, issue of *The Mining Journal*—goes like this: Thursday afternoon, October 19, 1939, Dockie Bowers and Charles Gustafson, known as Blind Charlie because of his poor eyesight, left the Burns dock in a small, wooden boat. They rowed out to fish at Black Rock Point, a dangerous promontory a little northwest of Big Bay. It juts out into the lake and often gets caught in shifting winds. They did not return. But, somewhat mysteriously, they were not reported missing until 10 a.m. on Saturday, October 21, 1939.

"A general alarm was raised," according to *The Mining Journal*, "and crews from Eagle Harbor and Portage stations assisted [the Marquette crew]."

Weather delayed the official searches, and the bodies were never recovered. However, the Coast Guard did locate two net boxes and nets about 300 yards off the shore of Big Bay. A few days later, on October 25, 1939, the Coast Guard found a badly damaged boat floating near Black Rock Point. They said it could have been the boat used by Bowers and Gustafson.

Dockie's family and friends also searched for him for weeks. As they did, more unofficial details of the trip emerged. Dockie was out lifting nets he had illegally set in the lake so probably had rowed out under the cover of darkness, and probably with a snoot full. He and his buddies often hauled in illegal catches of fish they would then sell to earn more cash to buy more liquor. They apparently drank and played a lot and worked only a little.

LIFTING NETS: Murdock (Dockie) Bowers, left, and Leo Doucette fish out of a small wooden boat launched from Burns Landing into Lake Superior, around 1938-9.
Family photo.

Dad and another of his younger brothers, Bill, nightly walked the six miles of the shoreline from Black Rock Point to the Big Bay Lighthouse searching for Dockie's remains. They even walked the entire shoreline from Big Bay to Marquette at one point. They always said they would know immediately if they found him—Dockie had a gold tooth front-center of his mouth. But his body never turned up.

Dad remained silent while Aunt Belle made her case. I knew he held his sister in higher regard than anyone; she was almost a mythical force, a woman who embodied generations of wisdom, authority, and resourcefulness from her hearty, female, peasant German ancestors. She was more a mother to him than a sister. He said Aunt Belle looked out for him from the time he was a young child. And even though my dad was now in his fifties, he obeyed her as a young boy does his mother.

Aunt Belle was the one he relied on for financial advice. She was the one he called when any of his kids were sick. My earliest memory is of Aunt Belle coming to the rescue when I was about three years old. My oldest sister had set me on the back fender of her bike and taken me for a spin. Somehow, my right foot got tangled in the spokes, and the flesh on my ankle was torn off clear to the bone. Aunt Belle made a honey plaster and wrapped it in her sterilized, handmade bandages. I still have a scar on my ankle, but that seemed like nothing considering how bad my sister felt.

Aunt Belle sponged my feverish face with a cool cloth all night when I had scarlet fever. Another time, while fighting with my sister, I put my arm through the glass in a cupboard door. Aunt Belle patched the gaping tear back together with her cowslip salve and butterfly bandages. Another time, she concocted a mustard in who-knows-what-else creamy substance she called a poultice and tied it to my foot with strips of an old sheet to draw out a huge splinter. It worked.

Aunt Belle, whose given name was Velma Fern, was born in Big Rapids, Michigan, on March 17, 1896. She was the fourth of fourteen kids. My dad, Claude Darius, born in 1902, was the eighth child. His family didn't say his middle name the way it is commonly pronounced today. They called him Claude DRY-us, which caused his big sister to lovingly nickname him Dry or Dry Ass. Murdock Oscar (Dockie), born in 1907, was the tenth in the lineup.

The American patriarch of the family, their grandfather, Friedrich Bauer, made his way from Germany to Michigan in the late 1850s. He homesteaded in the Big Rapids area of the Lower Peninsula of Michigan. One of his two sons, Robert Lorenzo (Wren), my dad's father, also ended up with a large homestead in the Big Rapids area. But times were tough, so Wren left his wife and younger kids to work the farm while he found a job in the booming lumber industry. The Brunswick Company brought him to Big Bay in 1910 to serve as a foreman of one of its logging camps. A six-foot-six-inch piece of rawhide, Wren was known as a ruthless ruler of his lumberjacks. It was said he refused to hire anyone whose ass he couldn't whip. He fathered fourteen children, nine boys and five girls. As the boys became old enough to work, they were forced to follow their father to the lumber camps, where, it is said, he "toughened" them up. Later, the oldest daughters, including Aunt Belle, became cooks at their dad's camps.

Their rugged, dangerous, and somewhat adventurous lives turned them into coarse characters with colorful, active imaginations. They all told great tall tales, but Aunt Belle's were the best.

She regularly regaled us with her stories while she performed her miracle cures on us or took us berry picking or taught us her kitchen skills.

One of my favorite stories was the mystery of the headless man. When Aunt Belle was still a young girl on the farm in Big Rapids,

CAMP 8: Robert Lorenzo (Wren) Bowers, second from left, served as foreman of the Brunswick Company's Camp No. 8 on the Big Pup Creek, near Big Bay. About 1912.
Family photo.

an older woman lived alone on a neighboring farm. The old woman paid a visit to my grandmother and said she was being visited nearly every night by an apparition—a man without a head paced back and forth on her front porch. She asked my grandmother to let Aunt Belle come stay with her to see if that might keep the ghost at bay.

My grandmother agreed and sent Aunt Belle to spend a few days with the frightened woman. Aunt Belle says she "stayed up the first night on the porch, real quiet, and that man without a head came. I secretly watched him for several nights and finally found the courage to ask him what he was doing there."

Aunt Belle says the headless man told her his wife had beheaded him and buried his body under an apple tree at the far end of the porch. The problem was, in the hurried cover-up, his head got tossed down by his feet, and he said he couldn't rest that way for eternity.

So, the next morning, Aunt Belle dug up the earth under that apple tree and indeed found a human skeleton. And sure enough, the head lay next to its feet. Aunt Belle carefully moved the head back to the top of the torso, and she threw the dirt back over the remains. The headless man never walked on the neighbor lady's porch again.

Some of the best stories were about the seances Aunt Belle attended with one or another of her sisters. Sometimes she would try to get in touch with my oldest brother, Claudie, who had died of polio at the age of eight in 1940. This would torture my poor mother, but I was captivated by the idea of communicating with those in the big beyond.

But most of the séances Aunt Belle attended were to try to connect with Dockie in the spirit world. She and two of her younger sisters, Lou and Mettie, went to the house of a spiritual medium in Muskegon in the mid-1950s. Aunt Belle said "the exotic-looking woman" closed the drapes and lit candles to create the proper atmosphere. Then all the ladies sat in a semi-circle, holding hands, all quiet as if they were sitting in church. Suddenly, they heard a loud "whoosh, whoosh," as if someone were coming to the surface of a lake, sucking for air. At the same time, the flames on the candles were snuffed out. "Oh, now I can breathe," a man sighed. And she knew it was Dockie.

My dad, I thought, was tormented by these stories and torn between his loyalty to Aunt Belle and his younger brother.

A bear of a man nearly six-feet tall, my dad acted tough—probably the way his father tried to rear him. But he was really a gentle, soft soul. He recited his favorite Longfellow poem to me when I was little—"Under a spreading chestnut tree,/The village smithy stands...." Or he would sing, off-key, "Tie Me to Your Apron Strings Again." And he was squeamish. We never had venison in our house, unlike all our relatives and friends. It was supposedly because he could not stand the smell of venison, but I think he couldn't bear

BOWERS BROOD: Several family members gather outside Gertie Bowers Beerman's house in Big Bay about 1950. From left: Gertie, Belle Bowers Burns, Claude Bowers, Lou Bowers Temple, and Vern Bowers. *Family photo.*

the thought of killing a deer. He did like to fish, but he couldn't clean his catch—my mother did that.

I could not imagine my dad digging up a cellar, looking for the body of his precious brother. But at the same time, I couldn't see him saying no to Aunt Belle, either.

But he tried. "Jesus, Jesus, Je-SUS CHRIST," he moaned in a songlike cadence rising to a crescendo on the second syllable of the third Jesus. "Belle, you're accusing Dockie's wife, who also happens to be your husband's niece, of murder. Think about that for a minute, would ya? You'd have to go to Aggie's uncles who still live in that house and tell them that. You know as well as I do that Dockie was no saint. And don't think all those guys don't know that—they were there for the drinking, carousing, brawls, and Christ himself knows what else. Don't you remember the time they were fooling around with their moonshine still and they got drunk and caught the beach on fire? You drove up to the Bay and got in a helluva fight with them.

"I didn't tell you, did I, about how he got me all mixed up in his bullshit doings the Christmas before he disappeared? The kids were just about to go to bed when I hear a knock at the back door. I swing it open, and there stands Dockie. He's grinning like a fool, so that gold tooth actually glowed. He was half-drunk, with no hat on that red-haired mop. He had been to Marquette the day before, got a belly full of liquor, and somehow swiped a bunch of presents for his kids and a toboggan to carry them. He walked the ten miles or so to Harlow Creek, pulling that thing. But it about wore him out, so he put it up over the snowbank and walked the rest of the way to Big Bay to get me to drive him back down there to pick up the Christmas presents for his kids."

Aunt Belle harumphed and said, "Well, you know Aggie was no better than he was. She drank enough to empty the lake, and if she had as many sticking out of her as she had stuck in her, she'd look like a goddammed porcupine. And why in hell did she wait for nearly three days to report him missing? That question has never, ever been answered, Dry Ass."

Dad was silent for a minute or so. Then he spoke quietly and haltingly, as if he were thinking out loud.

"You know as well as I do, Belle, that Dockie would take a knapsack with a bedroll and disappear in the woods for three days and as long as a week or more. He was as good a woodsman as any. The way those streams up through that way run full of brook trout, he could catch his supper in fifteen, twenty minutes, build a fire, and cook them. Maybe Aggie thought he was off in the woods."

I must've fallen asleep because that's the last I remember of that conversation. And I know I couldn't directly ask my dad about it—

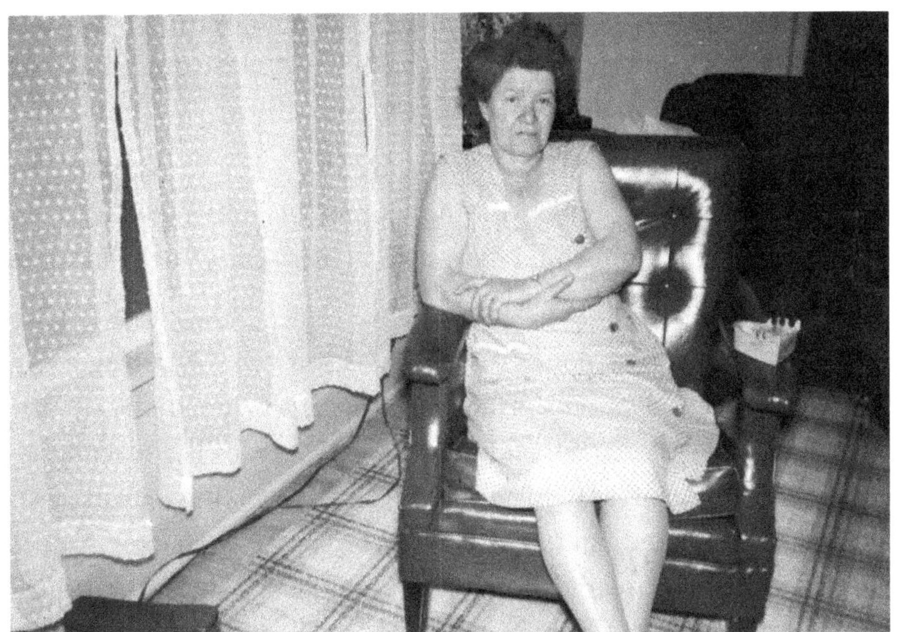

HOLDING COURT: Aunt Belle, about 1955, at home on the Big Bay Road, near Raish's Sawmill. *Family photo.*

he'd know I had been eavesdropping again. The subject of Dockie— or anything controversial relating to the family—was strictly taboo. But I worried that bossy Aunt Belle would convince him to dig up that cellar.

She exuded self-confidence and was a bit of a bully. Just a couple of months before this cellar conversation, Dad dropped me off at her house down by Raish's Mill to help her pack up her car—we were going to pick blueberries together up on Hogsback Mountain.

But I had to wait for her because a tall, thin electrician had just arrived at her house to repair her kitchen stove. Dressed in his dark blue work uniform, the timid man pulled the stove out a little from the wall. Aunt Belle, in her housedress and chunky-heeled, black shoes, stood with her hands planted on her hips. "You've gotta pull that stove out a helluva lot farther than that," she barked at the repairman. He shook his head, indicating he had plenty of room.

Aghast, she said much more insistently and loudly, "I said pull it out farther because I'm going to get back there with you so the next goddamned time it breaks, I can fix it myself."

I sat quietly at her kitchen table, a little embarrassed that she would speak that way, but also a little impressed that my elderly aunt would get on the floor behind that stove to learn the mechanics of an electric range.

After the job was done, we packed up a box of her amazing homemade treats. We made sandwiches from the bread that, by the smell of it, had only recently left her oven. There was her specialty— ground-up bologna, onion, and pickles, mixed with mayonnaise. There was egg salad, and my dad's favorite sandwiches with liver sausage, as well as a large pan of potato salad. We squeezed lemons for fresh lemonade, and packed up her homemade sponge cake with fresh strawberries. This went into the car, as well as our pails to pick berries—emptied-out, two-pound coffee cans with holes punched in the upper sides with a piece of wire strung through them to create a handle.

On the two-mile drive to my house, she told me about her last blueberry-picking trip. She had been up to Big Bay a few days before to pick with two of her sisters, Gertie and Lou. They had driven up on the plains on the graveled Triple A Road and found the promised land of blueberry patches, where they could plop down on the ground and pick all around them for the afternoon. The women then brought their coffee cans filled with sumptuous berries back to Gertie's kitchen where they began to wash, sort, and divide them.

Gertie's husband, Joe, three sheets to the wind, walked in while the sisters worked. Gertie gave Joe a look that would have withered a green plant and called him a useless son of a bitch. Which he was, according to Aunt Belle. She said their dad even thought so, because when Gertie—the oldest of the Bowers children—came home to announce that she was going to marry Joe, Wren said, "Well, all I'm getting you for a wedding present is a looking glass and washboard so you can watch while you work yourself to death."

FAMILY FUN: Joe Beerman, left, who married Gertie Bowers; Hattie Bowers, wife of Wren and mother of 14 children; Velma Fern (Belle) Bowers Burns; and Patty Burns at Burns Landing on Lake Superior, about 1916.
Family photo.

Joe grabbed the pan of berries out of Gertie's hand, ran to the back porch, and tossed the berries out in the driveway. Lou chased after him and hauled off and smacked him on the side of his head, knocking him off the porch. Aunt Belle said she followed and stood over him while Lou gathered up the berries. "Don't you dare get up, you stupid son of a bitch, because I'll knock you clear into next week if you even try."

Those conversations are my last memories of Aunt Belle. That fall, she moved to Albuquerque, New Mexico, to live near her daughter's family. As she was returning for a visit to Michigan in the spring of 1962, she suffered a fatal heart attack in Wisconsin.

HOMEWARD BOUND: Patty, Lois (their granddaughter), and Belle Bowers Burns prepare to leave Albuquerque, New Mexico, 1962. *Family photo.*

Fast forward nearly sixty years. I retired from a career in journalism on the East Coast and returned to Big Bay. The local township supervisor asked me if I could write a few paragraphs about the history of the Burns family's property, which was now owned by Powell Township. The property—now referred to as Burns Landing— had been turned into a public park, and the township rehabbed the only building that remained on the property, the original square log house built in the 1870s by Morris LeClaire.

While I researched the convoluted Burns-LeClaire family history, these memories of Uncle Dockie, married to Agnes (Aggie) Burns, came up, as well as the stories told by Aunt Belle, who was married to Patrick (Patty) Burns. Patty, it turns out, was both an uncle and brother-in-law to Aggie.

After Aunt Belle died, I don't remember much discussion of either the cellar theory or Dockie's demise. Sometimes, when my dad got together with some of his brothers or sisters, they'd reminisce briefly about him, but they never did want us kids to listen.

When I ask the old-timers who remain, including siblings and first cousins, all they remember are snippets of facts, stories, and theories.

I'm still left with more questions than answers. Was my aunt unable to accept a cherished brother's death by drowning? Did her seemingly endless pursuit of a clear answer through investigation, spiritualism, and religion cause her to confuse her ghost story of the headless man in some way with that of her brother? Can she and my dad, like the headless man, rest in eternity if they don't know what happened to their brother?

And I wonder why, after all this time, no skeleton with a gold tooth has ever washed ashore. Some say Lake Superior is so cold that it never gives up its dead. Maybe. But on the other hand, has anyone ever thought about searching that cellar?

In the Beginning: The LeClaire and Burns Families

BEFORE THERE WAS a town of Big Bay, and even before Powell Township existed, the LeClaire and Burns families lived on the shores of the natural harbor for which the town was named. Their spot on the shoreline was then—and for a long time after—known as Squaw Beach, but it is now more appropriately referred to as Burns Landing.

Big Bay's history is inextricably linked with these families because they were integral to the area's development. But like most Native American history in this country, much of theirs has been lost due to a lack of extensive record-keeping and objective, reliable storytelling.

Long before this country's lumber barons discovered the timber-rich forests along Lake Superior's southern shore, Native Americans fished and hunted in this region. They navigated it both by canoes on the "Big Lake" and a trail that ran from the West end of Lake Independence, a little inland, but along Lake Superior to L'Anse. They inhabited this land for hundreds, if not thousands, of years, according to several historians.

The first recorded histories begin in the mid-1600s, when French missionaries traveled through this region. Soon after, fur traders arrived and brought with them voyageurs—mixed French-Canadian and Native American boatmen and woodsmen who helped the fur traders travel through the dense countryside and transport their goods.

Then, Frederic Baraga, a missionary and Roman Catholic priest who would study and write about Native American languages, arrived in Michigan's Upper Peninsula to convert the Ojibwa to Catholicism. In 1843, he established the first mission at L'Anse. He called it Assinins (pronounced Ah-sin-ins), named after the local chief at the time, Edward Assinins. The site grew to include a church, orphanage, school, and houses.

Johann Georg Kohl, a German geographer, ethnologist, and travel writer, describes canoeing with Father Baraga to Assinins in 1855 in his book, *Kitchi-Gami: Life Among the Lake Superior Ojibway.**

> We…paddled still deeper into that purse-end of the gulf, until we sighted the little Catholic mission, with the Protestant mission lying on the other side of the bay, where it is only three miles in width.
>
> The former was our destination and we soon saw the brown population collected on the shore—men, women, children, and a countless pack of dogs. The bell of the little wooden church, built in the center of the village on a mound, began ringing hastily as soon as we came in sight. A flag was hoisted on a tall flagpole, and the guns of the young men were repeatedly discharged. When we landed, they all fell on their knees and received the blessing of their spiritual father.

*Note: The Native Americans who live mainly in northern Michigan and Ontario are today most often referred to as Ojibwa, which is the French variation of the name and what I use. But there are different spellings: Ojibwe, Ojibway, also Chippewa—the Anglicized form of the same word. The Ojibwa originated from a larger Algonquian-speaking ancestral group known as Anishinaabe.

ASSININS MISSION: The church, school, and orphanage
that made up the Catholic Mission near Baraga, early 1900s.
Photo from familysearch.org.

For several months in 1855, Kohl studied the lifestyle and customs of the Ojibwa, living among them at L'Anse and in northern Wisconsin. Unlike many white authors of the time, or the religious leaders who tried to turn them into whites, he writes more objectively and with an appreciation for Ojibwa practices.

This group of Ojibwa he approached on the shore at L'Anse likely included the LeClaire family, who were residents of the mission as well as some of the first Ojibwa to settle in what is now Big Bay. Records show they frequented both locations.

Morris LeClaire, sometimes referred to as Maurice or Mauritius LeClaire, was a French-Indian voyageur born in 1848. LeClaire traveled frequently between L'Anse and Big Bay to fish and hunt, likely years before he built the first square log cabin on the beach there in 1865, according to Fred Rydholm, who collected old-timers' accounts of events for years.

Later, in the 1870s, "he built a beautiful, two-storied hewn log house which remains there today," Rydholm writes in his two-volume tome about the Upper Peninsula, *Superior Heartland: A Backwoods*

History. That cabin was rehabbed by Powell Township and stands alone on the Burns Landing site today, which is now a public park owned and maintained by Powell Township.

ORIGINAL LOG HOME: 1940s photo of the two-story home built by Morris LeClaire and Charles Burns.
Photo courtesy of James Cherrette.

Morris was the oldest child of Francis LeClaire, a French Canadian, and Mary Cloutier, a member of the Ojibwa; he was half French and half Ojibwa of the L'Anse Band, from the Keweenaw Peninsula of Michigan, according to Kay Burns Duncan, his great-granddaughter who has extensively researched the family's history. Moreover, his family is listed as the thirty-third family baptized by Father Baraga at Assinins.

MORRIS LECLAIRE: The French/Indian voyageur who
built the original homes on Burns Landing in Big Bay.
Photo courtesy of Kay Burns Duncan.

```
29. Joannes Hotley (jun.Bonneterre)
    Anna Madjidjiwanokwe, uxor eius      1824           yes        yes

        Joanna, filia eorum              1845           yes        yes
      · Martha, filia eorum              1847 ·         yes        yes
        Joannes, filius eorum            1851
        Caecilia, filia eorum            1854           mortua     y
        Isabella, filia eorum            1856           yes
        Mathilda, filia orum             1859

    Caecilia Wabanokwe,mater Annae Madjidjiwanokwe
                                         1800           yes        yes
    Carolus Nitamigijig, filius Caec. Wab.    1833
    Jakobus, filius Joannes Hotley and Anna   1862


30. Daniel Kebeiassing                   1826           yes        mortuus
    Sophia Nawananikwe, uxor eius        1830           yes        yes

        Geoagius                         1847 - 1861    yes
        Susanna                          1852           yes        yes
        Katharina                        1854           ges
        Elizabeth                        1857-1859
        Elizabeth                        1869-1861
        Margarita                        1864
        Francisca,soror Sophia Nawan.    1853           yes


31. Eduardus Metakosige                                 yes        yes
    Ludovica Tibishkwaiabanokwe,uxor ej.1839           yes        yes

        Joanna, filia eorum              1858-1858
        Joannes Metakosige,pater Eduard 1795            mort.      yes
        Ludovicus,filius supradict.      1859-1860
        Eduardys,filius supradict.       1861
        Susanna,filia supradictorum      1864           mortua
        Suasnna,filia eorum              1866


32. Franciscus Xav. Le Clair             1820           yes        ges
    Maria Cloutier,uxor eius             1828           yes        yes

        Petrus Forcier,adoptatus ab eis 1847            yes
        Mauritius,filius                 1848           yes
        Franciscus,filius                1850           yes        yes
        Rosalia,filia                    1856           yes
        Antonius                         1858-1859      mortuus
        Antonius                         1860           mortuus
        Georgius,filius                  1862           mortuus
        Maria,filia                      1865
        Angelica Forcier,ddoptata ab eis 1855


33. Mauritius Chalifoux                  1819           yes        yes
    Margarita Cloutier,uxor eius         1832           yes        yes
        FRanciscus Xav,filius            1849
        Petrus,filius                    1853
        Benjamin                         1855-1859
        Joannes                          1859
        Simeon                           1861
```

BAPTISM RECORD: Francis LeClaire and his family were among the earliest members of the Ojibwa community at Baraga to be baptized by Bishop Frederic Baraga. They were the 33rd family baptized as shown here, on page 8, of *The Book of Baptisms*, St. Ann's Church, Assinins. *Record from familysearch.org.*

84. Thomas McGillen		yes	yes
Bridget, uxor eius		yes	yes
Anna	1865	yes	yes
Edward	1867	yes	yes
Mary	1868	yes	yes
Margaret	1869	yes	yes
Louisa	1871		
Alice	1874		
Henry	1876		
85. Edward Auger	1856	yes	yes
Anna , uxor eius	1861	yes	yes
86. Francis Migisins	1855	yes	
Agatha, uxor eius	1850	yes	yes
Cecilia, filia eorum	1868	yes	yes
87. Gabriel Forcier	1849	yes	yes
Martha, uxor eius	1854	yes	yes
Alexander	1866	yes	yes
John	1876		
Cecilia	1874		
88. Mauritius LeClair	1856	yes	yes
Jane, uxor eius	1857	yes	yes
Thresia	1870		
Francis	1873		
Margaret	1876		
89. Johannes Hand		yes	yes
Bridget, uxor eius		yes	yes
Catherine	1867	yes	yes
William	1869	yes	yes
Thomas	1871		
Henry	1875		
Louisa 1	1877		
90. Joseph Peter Golbach		yes	yes
Mary, uxor eius		yes	yes
Jacob	1870		
Peter	1873		
91. Bernard Mettner		yes	yes
Philomena, uxor eius		yes	yes
92. George Manitogijig		yes	yes
Maria, uxor eius	1858	yes	yes
93. Joseph Sandeline	1853	yes	yes
Hariet, uxor eius	1857	yes	yes
Julia	1871		
Isidor	1873		
Edward	1875		
95. Michael Piagigebi	1858	yes	yes
Maria, uxor eius	1863	yes	yes
Maria, filia eorum	1877		

BAPTISM RECORD: The Mauritius (Morris) LeClaire family was the 88th family baptized by Bishop Frederic Baraga at Assinins; here they are listed on page 16 of the *Book of Baptisms*, St. Ann's Church, Assinins. *Record from familysearch.org.*

The LeClaires are even mentioned in Bishop Frederic Baraga's diary. "Aug. 12 — Today Leclair's small boy burned himself. The best remedy is, butter, incense, gaume [a gum or resin]," Father Baraga wrote on August 12, 1852. The footnote in *The Diary of Bishop Frederic Baraga*, edited and annotated by Regis M. Walling and Rev. N. Daniel Rupp, says "LeClair" is Francis LeClair, who was Morris' father. The little boy who suffered the burns might well have been Morris, who would have been about four years old at the time, or possibly his younger brother, Francis, who would have been two years old.

Morris LeClaire married Jane Mataxagay, who was a full Ojibwa, also from the L'Anse band. Together, they had at least four children, all of whom were born in Baraga County and who were one-fourth French and three-fourths Ojibwa, records show. Theresa Rose LeClaire was born between 1867-70; George was born September 7, 1872; Margaret (Maggie) LeClaire was born June 12, 1875; and Daniel LeClaire was born March 31, 1878. Morris' wife and children were the eighty-eighth family baptized by Father Baraga at the mission at L'Anse.

Whether the family canoed over to the Big Bay area to fish in summers only, or spent more of the year in Big Bay, is not clear. It is likely, though, that they routinely traveled between the two places. All of Morris' children were born in Baraga County, or at least the births were recorded by the mission there. The 1880 US Census shows the family lived in Baraga County. But the 1900 US Census shows they lived at the beach in Big Bay.

During the years LeClaire built the log houses on Squaw Beach, not long after the Civil War ended, lumber barons and land developers, too, began to arrive in Big Bay. That likely provided work for LeClaire, who was known as an excellent guide, fisherman, and timberman.

"Several Marquette residents bought tracts of land in what is now Powell Township but little logging was done for some time," according to "Historical Highlights—Big Bay," an early, undated paper from the Marquette County Historical Society. "In 1877 and 1878, some Quebec capitalists interested in cutting and processing white pine…called for clear white pine timbers, squared and as long as possible and local jobbers [to] cut it." The paper goes on to say that supplies were ferried by scows from Marquette to the Yellow Dog and Salmon Trout Rivers since this was before a road or railroad existed between Marquette and Big Bay. In addition, "some French-Canadian lumberjacks were imported to help get out logs and square them."

The squaring of the logs was necessary so they would not roll when they were rafted from the mouths of the rivers near Big Bay to Marquette. From there, they were loaded on special vessels to accommodate the huge logs. These ships carried the squared logs to lumberyards along the St. Lawrence River, and some made it to as far away as Europe.

Also, not long after LeClaire built his log homes on the beach at Big Bay and the lumbering business began to grow, probably in 1883 or 1884, Charles (Charlie) Burns joined the family. He likely connected with LeClaire through their work. Both Burns and LeClaire are listed as timbermen, guides, and fishermen on various US Census and other official records.

Charlie eventually married into the LeClaire family, beginning the extended Burns line, some of whom remain in the area today. He and Morris LeClaire built several more dwellings at Burns Landing, in addition to their dock used for fishing and offloading goods and people. Over the years, other docks were built nearby, as it was basically the only way to get anything in and out of Big Bay.

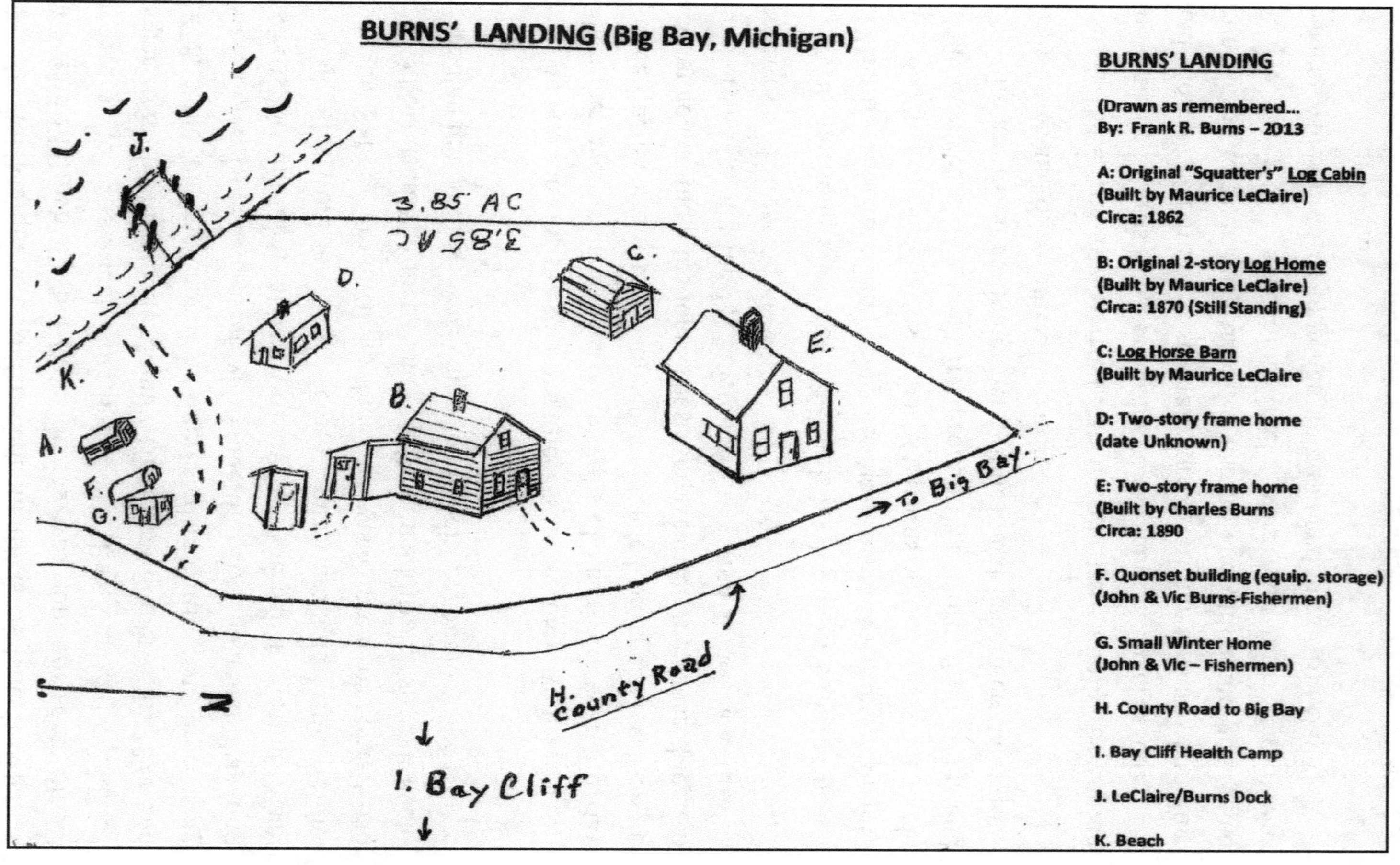

BURNS' LANDING

(Drawn as remembered...
By: Frank R. Burns – 2013

A: Original "Squatter's" Log Cabin
(Built by Maurice LeClaire)
Circa: 1862

B: Original 2-story Log Home
(Built by Maurice LeClaire)
Circa: 1870 (Still Standing)

C: Log Horse Barn
(Built by Maurice LeClaire

D: Two-story frame home
(date Unknown)

E: Two-story frame home
(Built by Charles Burns
Circa: 1890

F. Quonset building (equip. storage)
(John & Vic Burns-Fishermen)

G. Small Winter Home
(John & Vic – Fishermen)

H. County Road to Big Bay

I. Bay Cliff Health Camp

J. LeClaire/Burns Dock

K. Beach

LEFT - BURNS LANDING: This 2013 map of the original dwellings to once exist on the family compound was drawn by Francis Burns, Jr., grandson of Charles Burns.
Photo courtesy of Kay Burns Duncan.

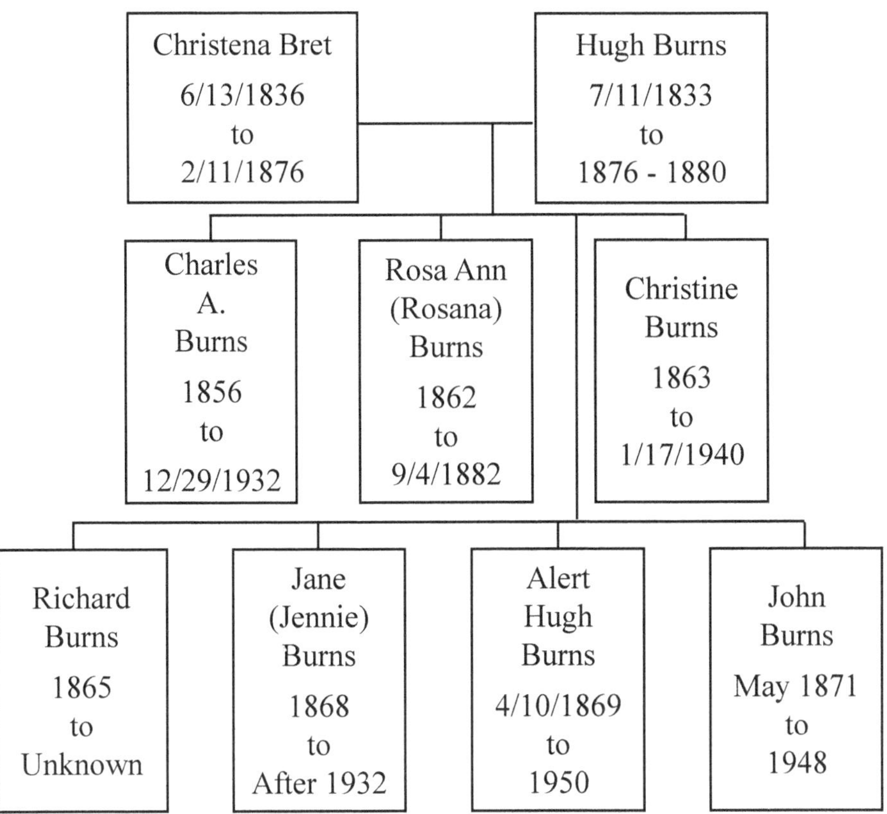

FAMILY TREE: Children of Hugh Burns and Christena Bret.

Charlie is believed to be the first white settler in Big Bay, who in his early years there earned a living by fishing in the summer and squaring timbers from pine for the lumber companies in the winter, according to Burns Duncan.

Charlie was also instrumental in the development of the community of Big Bay, as well as the creation of Powell Township. He held many early, important jobs such as ferrying mail between Marquette and Big Bay—by boat in summer and dogsled in winter. Charlie was among the early petitioners who lobbied Marquette County to create Powell Township. He was one of the first appointed board members for the newly created Powell Township and for the Powell Township School Board. As a highway commissioner, Charlie helped develop the first modern road between Marquette and Big Bay and improve many other roads throughout the township.

Born to Hugh and Christina (Bret) Burns in Upper Canada in about 1856, Charles Burns was the eldest of seven children. His father, who had been born in Ireland, was a fisherman, which may be the reason the family emigrated to Marquette, Michigan, in 1868, Burns Duncan says.

The 1870 US Census shows the Burns family resided in Marquette. Charlie's mother, Christena Bret Burns, who was of Scottish descent, died on February 11, 1876, in Marquette. Charlie's father, Hugh, apparently died sometime before 1880 as well since there is no mention of him in the 1880 census. And Charlie told his children, Burns Duncan says, that he and his siblings had been orphaned and separated when they were young.

The US Census for 1880 shows Charlie and his sister, Christine, lived with the Elizabeth Lavelly family in Marquette. Charlie would have been about twenty-four then, and Christine would have been fourteen.

In 1884 or 1885, Charlie married Rosa (Rosalie) LeClaire, in an Ojibwa ceremony, according to Burns Duncan. Rosa was a sister to Morris LeClaire. She and Charlie had no children, and in 1885 they divorced, Indian custom, which means the couple separated and never resumed marital relations.

Rosa, when she left Charlie, returned to Assinins. She died there on February 20, 1886, and is buried in the Assinins cemetery.

EARLY YEARS: Theresa LeClaire Burns leads a horse
away from the square log barn, built by her father and
husband at Burns Landing.
Photo courtesy of Kay Burns Duncan.

On July 6, 1886, Charlie married his second wife, Theresa Rose
LeClaire, in Marquette, Michigan. The oldest daughter of Morris and
Jane Mataxagay LeClaire, Theresa is listed as sixteen years old on the
record and Charlie as twenty-seven. The record also shows a priest
married the couple. Theresa and Charlie lived at Burns Landing,
where Theresa gave birth to four children: Joseph Burns was born
December 22, 1886; James H. Burns on August 6, 1888; Albert H.
Burns on July 30, 1890; and Christine Burns on February 10, 1892.

Charlie obtained a divorce from Theresa, on grounds of desertion,
on November 12, 1900. She, too, had left Big Bay and returned to
the mission near L'Anse. She died on June 5, 1916, at the St. Joseph
Catholic Mission at Assinins and is buried in the Assinins cemetery.

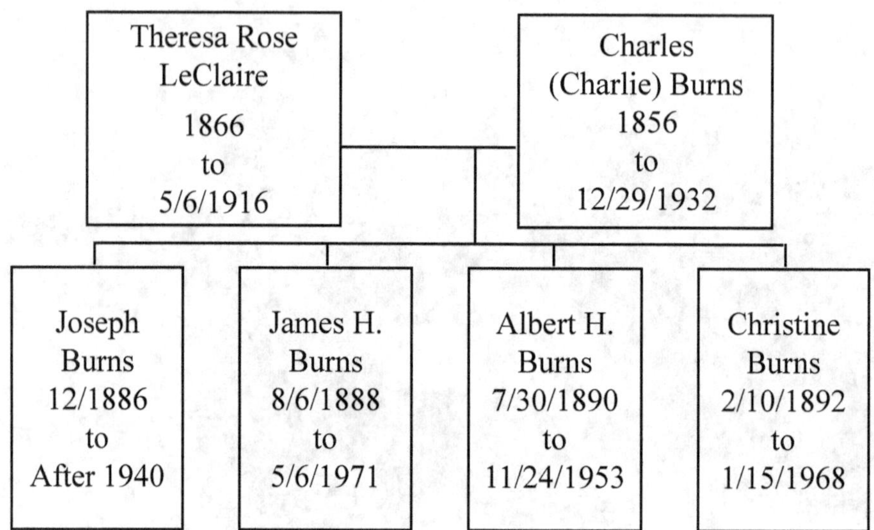

CHARLES AND THERESA TREE:
The two had four children together.

Although there is no official record, the Justice of the Peace in Big Bay married Charlie and Margaret (Maggie), Theresa's younger sister in 1898, according to Burns Duncan. (They were later married by a Catholic priest on May 26, 1922.) Maggie, too, had been previously married. She married Michael Montgomery, also an Ojibwa from L'Anse, on June 6, 1892, in Marquette. Both were residents of Big Bay at the time, the record states. They had one son, Patrick, born January 2, 1896. According to Rydholm, Montgomery walked off one day and never returned. Margaret later, on July 11, 1898, gave birth to an illegitimate daughter, Mary Jane, in Baraga.

Together, Charlie and Maggie raised his four oldest children from his marriage to Theresa, Maggie's two children, who adopted the last name Burns, and went on to have eight more children together, all born at Burns Landing: Charles John (Johnny), born April 11, 1902; Margaret Bertha, born July 14, 1904; Francis Edward (Frank), born August 6, 1906; Victor David, born July 1, 1908; Albena M., born August 31, 1910; Forrest Elden (Flossie), born August 24, 1912; Eva Alice, born August 29, 1915; and Jennie, born June 12, 1917.

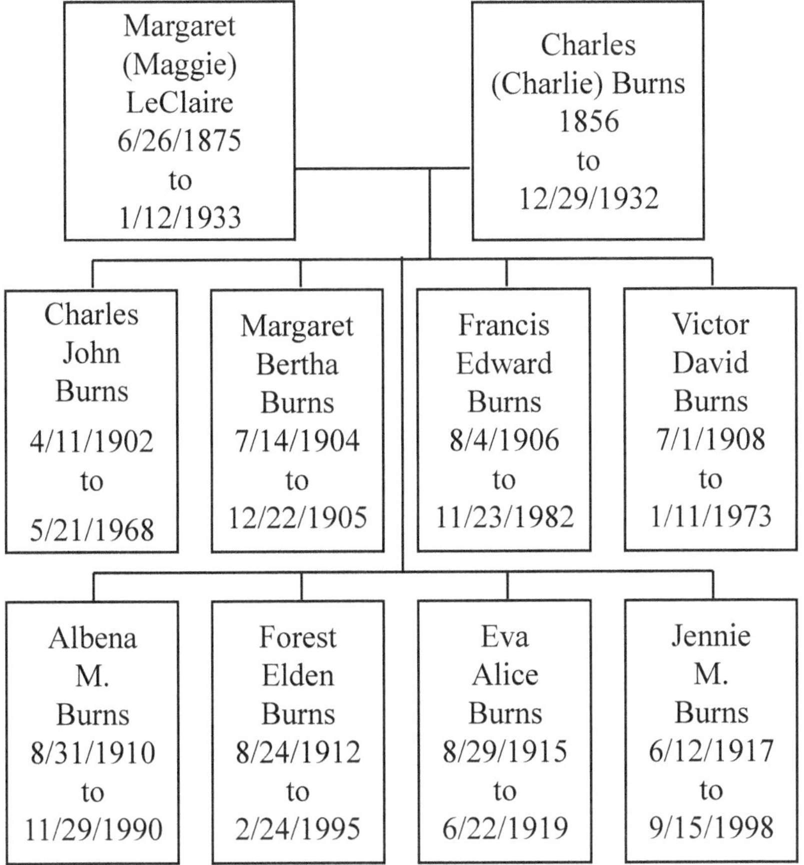

CHARLES AND MARGARET (MAGGIE) TREE:
The two had eight children together.

As the Burns-LeClaire family grew, so too did the area that surrounded them. Timber, mineral, and land developers had arrived in the Marquette area in the mid-nineteenth century. Marquette was officially created as a village in the fall of 1849. By 1900, Marquette was a thriving city, a center of shipping for the Upper Peninsula, with rail links, and a population of 11,500.

Businessmen began to reach out into the surrounding areas, especially lumbermen and land developers such as Peter White and Daniel Powell, among many others.

FAMILY TIME AT BURNS LANDING:
Margaret (Maggie) LeClaire Burns, left, holding Forest
(Flossy) Burns; Francis (Frank) Burns, the first child
baptized in Powell Township; Albena M. Burns; and
Christine Burns. About 1911-12.
Photo courtesy of Kay Burns Duncan.

One of the area's more well-known industrialists was John Munro
Longyear, an American businessman who purchased and developed
a great deal of timber and mineral lands in the Upper Peninsula.
Mr. Longyear writes in his *Reminiscences*, held at the Marquette
Regional History Center, about many of his early contributions to
the area, which include:

- In 1892, in collaboration with Horatio Seymour, Peter White,
  and others, he helped establish the Huron Mountain Club, an
  exclusive, private pleasure club built along the mouth of the
  Pine River on Lake Superior near Big Bay. The HMC is still
  active today.

- In 1893, Longyear bought a small steamer, *The City of New Baltimore*, to ferry guests of the HMC and others between Marquette, the Huron Mountain Club, and Huron Bay, which is about twenty miles northwest of the HMC. Two years later, he bought a bigger steamship to enlarge his operation.

- In 1898, because of his success with the HMC and to increase numbers for his steamship operation, Longyear established Camp Sosowagami (Soso), another private club, at the mouth of the Yellow Dog River at Lake Superior. That property was eventually turned into a boys' camp and finally sold to a private party. "I was so occupied with other matters that I was unable to give the forming of a new club much attention and turned it over to others to do," Longyear writes. "I have tried several times spasmodically to rehabilitate the Soso enterprise but was never able to give it enough consecutive effort to accomplish anything."

Longyear's *Reminiscences* don't include specific discussion of the LeClaires or Charles Burns. But records show that Longyear interacted with both the Ojibwa living on the beach at Big Bay and with Charles Burns. Longyear writes in his diary about a stop at Burns Landing and his discussions with the Ojibwa living there, and, most likely, with Charlie Burns.

Charlie worked for Longyear as a "bushwacker" as evidenced by a photograph Longyear himself took of him in 1886, the only known photo of Charlie to exist today.

In July 1889, Longyear and some of his associates left Marquette on his launch called the *Abbie* to fish and explore along the shores of Lake Superior. Later, in about 1910, he put together a scrapbook of his recollections and photos, which he presented to his daughter, for whom his launch was named.

On the first day out, Longyear describes their approach to the beach in Big Bay in the journal he kept during the trip.

[A]s we approached the west end of the sand-beach, stretching across the south end of the bay, a small, temporary landing gradually detached itself from the masses of drift-wood piled on the beach and a few log huts were soon visible among the trees, the whole forming a fisherman's home, or station, of which we were to see many during the voyage. A year before a chart-case had been lost from the Abbie in Big Bay and the fisherman having sent word that he had found it, a short call was made here during which it was produced and restored to its old place in the launch.

A number of Indians, some of them apparently very old, were scattered about and were looked at with much interest by some of the crew whose acquaintance with the fast-disappearing aborigines was limited. As none of the visiting members of the crew happened to be smokers, their failure to respond to the request for "see-mah," (tobacco), apparently caused the red brother, and sister, to regard their white brothers with great indifference. The crew were chiefly interested in a couple of Indians, a man and a woman, evidently very old, who were squatted on the bare ground in the dusty path between two of the houses. They scarcely moved and seemed to be content to sit on the warm earth in the sunshine, and just breathe.

"Are they alive?" It was the engineer who spoke. He came from New York and had not seen Indians.

The boats had recently returned from the nets and as we were pushing off, one of the fishermen threw a three-pound whitefish into the launch, which was accepted with thanks, our fishermen not yet having had an opportunity to show their skill in filling the larder.

BUSHWACKERS: John M. Longyear in 1886 photographed
Charles Burns, left, and Harry McGrath, who worked for
him in the Ives Lake and Huron Mountain Club areas.
Photo courtesy of The Marquette Regional History Center.

The fisherman Longyear mentions most likely was Charlie Burns, as they had previously worked together, and the location is clearly Burns Landing. Longyear's descriptions of the Ojibwa, the LeClaires, he encountered on the beach perhaps sound insensitive today, but that is typical language used by white explorers and developers of the time. Longyear goes on to describe sailing on for the Huron Mountain Club, where he encountered more Ojibwa from L'Anse. Longyear writes:

> We had been told at Big Bay that there was plenty of water for the Abbie to cross the bar at the mouth of Pine River, so, it was decided to stop there for the night. We ran along under the bluffs and cliffs of red sandstone on the west side of Big Bay; past Salmon-Trout River Point; across Salmon Trout Bay, which receives the river of the same name, the Speckled trout fishing of which has furnished material for many a tale of big catches; past point Conway and Pine River Point. All these points are "Red-heads," the cliffs of which look out over the widest part of Lake Superior, from heights of fifty to one hundred feet. After passing the last-named point we entered the wide, shallow bay, with its long stretch of yellow sand beach into which Pine River pours its dark flood, and the launch headed for low sand-dunes which mark the river's mouth…. We also discovered an Indian camp near us, containing a family from the mission at L'Anse, twenty-five miles up the coast. Their conveyance was a bark canoe. They were after birch bark, which grows here in abundance, peels readily at this season and is put by the squaws to many varied uses. Birch bark is a regular and very necessary part of the annual harvest of the aborigines.

As Native Americans, the LeClaires may not have thought of applying to the US government for ownership of the land they lived on; their culture didn't entertain the concept of land ownership. As Longyear indicates, fishing stations were built up all along the coast between Big Bay and L'Anse, where members of the Ojibwa regularly fished and hunted.

COLLECTING BIRCH BARK: Ojibwa women from the mission near Baraga canoe to Pine River, now located within the Huron Mountain Club, to gather birch bark for a myriad of uses. Photo taken by John M. Longyear in 1889. *Photo courtesy of The Marquette Regional History Center.*

But on June 28, 1897, Charles Burns purchased the land his growing family lived on at Burns Landing from William Busch, another lumber baron, according to a deed for the property registered at the Marquette County Register of Deeds.

Rydholm and others say around this time a stone dock was built on the bay, just west of the LeClaire/Burns dock. Various other records provide evidence of some of that early, industrial activity that led to the area's growth.

- From 1888 to 1890, John H. Gillette, a Marquette lumber dealer who also operated a tugboat business, purchased 270 acres from the Newport and Lake Superior Land Company and opened a brownstone quarry just west of the mouth of the Salmon Trout River. He reportedly employed about eighty men and constructed a boardinghouse, a blacksmith shop, stable, and other structures, as well as a stone dock riprapped by excess brownstone that wasn't salable, according to H. James Bourque and Associates, who in 1999 published a stone feasibility study of the area.

- In 1898, the McAfee brothers from Grand Rapids purchased 12,000 acres of timber southwest of Lake Independence and engaged Gus Anderson from Marquette to expand the dock on the west end of Burns Landing. This was begun in the winter of 1899 and finished the following summer, according to Betty A. Waring, who authored three short books about the area.

- In 1901, the McAfee Brothers, with financial backers from the East Coast, established the Big Bay Lumber Company— the first known use of the name Big Bay—with $1,000,000 in capital. The McAfees dismantled a mill they owned at Lakeview, in Lower Michigan, and shipped it to Marquette. From there, the mill was transported by scow, a flat-bottomed barge designed to haul huge equipment, to the dock at Burns Landing and then reassembled on the northwest corner of Lake Independence. They planned to cut the remaining white pine, as well as virgin hemlock, birch, basswood, cedar, and elm, according to Waring.

As the lumber industry expanded, people seeking work began to flow into the area. In 1900, when she was two years old, Cora Beerman LaRouche, along with her family, moved to Burns Landing to live in one of the LeClaire/Burns log cabins. Cora says her family, along with a few head of cattle they owned, walked from Marquette to Big Bay on a rudimentary dirt road that followed the Lake Superior shore. Cora goes on to say that their remaining belongings were sent by boat from Marquette to Big Bay. Waring published Cora's memories in *The Story of Lake Independence.*

Cora fondly remembers the Ojibwa children she played with at her temporary home on the beach, and says the Burnses and LeClaires invited her family to attend several special celebrations, when other members of the Ojibwa tribe would canoe over from L'Anse. They would feast and dance, Cora says, in a big clearing by the lake.

Cora also recalls her playmates' mother, Maggie Burns, who made moccasins from deerskins her children had stretched and softened. And she remembered Maggie's "very neat house and the huge batches of bread she baked for the large Burns family."

The reference to hard-working women is common in many cultures, especially among pioneer women, but it was particularly relevant in the Ojibwa society.

Kohl, the German ethnologist and travel writer who lived among the Ojibwa for months, wrote extensively about his observations of the traditions practiced by the Ojibwa women.

Kohl says when he first arrived to live among them, he needed to build his own wigwam and kindle his own fire. He was assigned an Ojibwa woman, the wife of a well-traveled voyageur, to act as his interpreter. He describes how they built the frame and covered the structure.

"This is the business of the women, and like all the work, heavy or light," it was their responsibility, he writes, with the "exception of hunting."

"My Indian woman went into the wood with an axe and felled the trees, and dragged them out. Her old mother and younger sister and her daughters helped her in the job...."

He goes on to describe the process of how they placed the trees—birch in this case, although they preferred tamarack—in the ground to form a quadrangle. They then bent the branches and twisted them together, and secured them with bast, a strong, threadlike twine created from Cedar. They then added crossbars, which creates an intricate arbor, Kohn explains, before they covered the structure with birch bark.

"With their short tobacco pipes in their mouths, and their children in wooden cradles on their backs," the women completed the wigwam, he writes.

"Besides building," he goes on to say, "they had many other matters to attend to; at times the old woman's pipe would go out, and she ran into the nearest hut to re-light it. Then a small boy came up, whose shirt was unfastened, and his clothes had to be tied up with a bit of the same bast employed on my mansion. Then they must look tenderly at their children, whom they had propped up against the trees, run up and kiss them, put their hands, ribbons or caps straight, or sit down for a minute on the grass, lost in the admiration of their little one.

"The women are also obliged to procure and cut up the firewood in the forest," Kohl continues. "This is one of their chief daily tasks, and in the neighbourhood of the Indian encampments around me I always hear at a certain hour in the evening the axes of the women and girls sounding as they prepare the logs for the next day, and emerge heavily laden from the scrub…. Their hands are much harder to the touch than the mens, and indeed their entire muscular system is far more developed, and they are proportionately stronger in the arm."

Cora's descriptions about how hard Maggie Burns worked and her early life at Burns Landing are among the few remaining tales of what life was like in Big Bay's infancy. Cora went on to say that soon after the Beermans arrived, her father, Prosper Beerman, was hired by the McAffee brothers to clear land for the mill they reassembled on the northwest shore of Lake Independence.

In addition to the mill, the McAffees' Big Bay Lumber Company built a bunkhouse, a cook shanty, about sixteen houses, a one-room schoolhouse, and a company store. All the buildings, making up a new town on the shore of Lake Independence, below the hill of the present town, were painted red. That is why, earlier residents say, that first settlement was called Red Town.

Morris LeClaire became the first-aid attendant at the mill, according to Burns Duncan. And in his later years, he became a janitor there.

According to Waring, Charles Burns, with his dog sled, delivered the first mail to Red Town in 1900. Prosper Beerman later took over the mail route from Burns, using a team and wagon, with an overnight stop at Saux Head Lake. The road, Waring says, at that time "followed the Lake Superior shoreline to Saux Head Lake, where there was a half-way house, to the north side of Lake Independence. It then followed along Squaw Beach and continued west to the Huron Mountain Club."

The lumber mill, the main source of employment for people in the town of Big Bay, experienced years of fortunes but misfortunes too. When lumber prices were up, it hummed along. When prices fell, the mill often shut down.

The mill burned down at least two times. It burned and shut down in 1902, for example, and remained closed until later in 1903, when it was rebuilt and remained in use until 1912, according to Waring.

"A report in 1904 by [manager of the mill W. B.] Ransom stated that Big Bay was one of the liveliest towns in the area; 130 men were working in the mill and three lumber camps, and 40,000 feet of hemlock and hardwood were cut daily. The dock at Burns Landing had been extended to 600 feet, and all of the lumber was being loaded and shipped from there as long as the big lake stayed open," Waring writes.

In 1905, the Marquette and Southeastern Railway Company extended its service to Birch, a village about halfway between Marquette and Big Bay, then on to Big Bay.

Two deals reportedly set up the transaction. Owners of the Northern Lumber Company purchased 20,000 acres of timberland that included Saux Head Lake from the Cleveland Cliffs Iron Company, with "the stipulation that the company's railroad, the Marquette and Southeastern, would be extended to Saux Head and Big Bay," according to Waring, in her book, *Birch, Michigan: Gold'n Memories*.

Moreover, the Big Bay Lumber Company agreed to transport its lumber by rail only if the service extended to Big Bay.

By November 1905, according to *The Mining Journal*, thirty-three buildings had been erected at Birch and the population was 300. By December of 1905, the Marquette and Southeastern Railroad had established regular runs, hauling wood products to Marquette. By 1909, the population had grown to 600—the highest point.

During this period of extensive growth, as the mill and ancillary enterprises began to operate and the population grew, the business stakeholders and the men who owned land and were able to vote,

MILL RENOVATION AND RED TOWN: This view
is looking West and the photo was taken in 1912, when
construction for the new mill started, according to Milton
Tompkins, Sr. The forms are for the line shafts in the mill. You
can see the remaining houses of Red Town off to the right.
Photo courtesy of Emmerson Fleury, Jr.

including Charles Burns, began to seek funds for the area's much-needed infrastructure. They first lobbied Marquette Township, and other townships that held land in what now makes up Powell Township, to appropriate funds from property taxes collected to build a reliable road from Marquette to Big Bay that would be passable year-round.

Discouraged with the lack of results, in February 1904 these businessmen and early settlers petitioned the Marquette County Board of Supervisors to create a new township. They argued the tax money collected on the properties within the new township, which they recommended be called either the Township of Big Bay or Superior, could then be used to pay for roads and other supportive infrastructure for the residents and businesses of the area.

After appointing a special committee to study the issue, the Marquette County Board of Supervisors, on March 28, 1904, officially created Powell Township. It was named after Dan Powell, one of the early lumber barons with operations in the Big Bay area, as well as a Marquette banker and long-time member of the Marquette County Board of Supervisors. Territory to make up the new township was taken from Marquette, Ishpeming, Champion, and Michigamme Townships, making Powell the largest township in Marquette County. In that same meeting, the Board of Supervisors named three electors to preside over Powell Township's upcoming meetings: Oscar Webster, Charles Burns, and John Nesbitt, early settlers in the area.

At the same time, Charles Burns was appointed to serve on the Powell Township Board of Education, along with W. B. Rasmussen and John W. Brown. Burns served on both boards for many years, often as treasurer, as well as on the highway commission, responsible for the road from Marquette to Big Bay and other access roads in the region.

State of Michigan,
County of _Marquette_ } ss.

I do Solemnly Swear, ...That I will support the
Constitution of the United States, and the Constitution of this State, and that I will discharge the duties
of _Treasurer of Powell Township_
according to the best of my ability.

Subscribed and sworn to before me, this _4th_
day of _April_ A. D. 19_06_

Charles Burns

W. N. Elliott
Clerk of Powell Twp.

State of Michigan,
County of _Marquette_ } ss.

I do Solemnly Swear, ...That I will support the
Constitution of the United States, and the Constitution of this State, and that I will discharge the duties
of _School Trustee_
according to the best of my ability.

Subscribed and sworn to before me, this _31_
day of _July_ A. D. 19_06_

Charles Burns

W. N. Elliott, Clerk

TOWNSHIP ROLES: Charles Burns was one of the early landowners who advocated for the creation of Powell Township in 1904. He then served on Powell Township's government board as well as on its school board. Copies of the oaths of office he signed are located within the Powell Township Board's minutes.

The Powell Township Board meeting minutes, as well as those of the PT School Board for the first year of its existence, are held at the PT Hall in Big Bay. The boards held their early meetings either at that one-room schoolhouse in Red Town or at the schoolhouse in Birch. Those records make clear that they took their jobs seriously and immediately began to tackle their goals.

Soon after the township's creation, the three PT board members met with the boards of the four townships from which Powell

Township was created. Those four townships handed over the tax monies they had collected from landowners now residing in Powell Township. With that, the PT Board began to conduct the township's business.

Within the first year of meeting records, the school board, with Charlie as treasurer, purchased new blackboards, desks with seats, and found a teacher for the one-room schoolhouse in Red Town.

The following year, in September 1906, the minutes show the school board accepted a bid for $1,720 to build a new, two-story schoolhouse at Birch, which was experiencing tremendous growth.

"By September 1906, 50 houses had been built and more were needed…. The population was 300, plus 250 men employed by the mill. In 1905, a schoolhouse had been built for the 43 children of school age in the area, but in September 1906, a large two-story school was built by Powell Township," Waring writes.

Waring goes on to say that the first Roman Catholic mission was opened at Birch in 1906, and on August 9, 1907, Father J. A. Sauriol baptized Francis Burns—son of Charlie—the first baptism there.

Burns Duncan remembers a story her father, Francis Burns, shared with her. "He told me that Maggie was Roman Catholic, and she raised her sons Catholic. But the daughters in the family went to Protestant services with their father, Charlie." From the early 1900s until 1931, when the Presbyterian Church was built in Big Bay, a traveling minister visited on weekends and held services in either the town hall or hotel. The Catholic mission set up at Birch served local Catholics until St. Mary's Catholic Church was built in Big Bay in 1919.

But Birch, in the way of other mill towns, didn't last long. Much of it, actually, was swallowed by Big Bay. First, the Brunswick Balke Collender Company purchased the Big Bay Lumber Company in 1908, and changed the mill's name to The Lake Independence Lumber Company.

The new company began to expand and create a new mill. In 1912, the Lake Independence Lumber Company purchased the Northern Lumber Company's 20,000 acres and the town of Birch. In October of that year, the mill at Birch was closed, disassembled, and moved to Big Bay to be incorporated in the construction of a new mill there, which was finished in 1914.

Between 1912 and 1926, when Jay Brunswick Deutsch became its president, The Lake Independence Lumber Company reportedly spent nearly $1 million to rebuild the mill and town. The new mill, incorporating the machinery from Birch, was constructed closer to the present town of Big Bay, and to make room for a larger yard to hold its lumber, it added nearly thirty houses up the hill from the mill, becoming the current town of Big Bay. The buildings in Red Town were either moved or torn down.

ENCAMPED AT BURNS LANDING: The story goes, when the Raymens first arrived in 1910, there was no room for them in Red Town so they had to wait for the town of Big Bay to be built. *Family photo.*

The Raymen family moved to Big Bay in 1910, during this revival of mill activity. Although the mill had begun to build the new homes on the hill, none were yet available for the Raymens, which by this time included married children and their partners, and a few young children. So the family lived in a large tent at the base of the dock at Burns Landing.

RAYMENS: Standing from left: Ray Raymen, Aby Dalton, xx, xx, Harry Mitchell, Florence Raymen Mitchell, Edith Raymen Murray, Jim Murray, William Hultz, Louella Raymen Hultz, Sarah Fonger Raymen. In front from left: Lester Hultz, Vera Hultz, May Raymen French with young Dorothy French Bowers. *Family photo.*

Peter Raymen, who became a sawyer at the mill, recalled later that those first summer nights were often stiflingly hot. He and some of his male family members slept on the Burns dock at night to enjoy the cool breezes off the lake.

The docks at Burns Landing, which served as the gateway to Big Bay for so long, were used much less frequently after the railroad was extended to Big Bay and even less after the newer road to Big Bay was built. They fell into disrepair and eventually disappeared.

BURNS COMPOUND: This view is from the top of the hill (Bay Cliff) looking east. Note the buildings below that made up the Burns compound. The log cabin in the center is now the only one that remains.
Photo courtesy of James Cherrette.

As the period of regrowth ensued, and the town moved up the hill, the Powell Township School Board recognized the need for a newer, more modern school. Powell Township built a new, two-story schoolhouse in the village of Big Bay in 1914. It was called the Charles Burns School, named after the man who had early on supported the new township's educational needs.

Unfortunately, that school burned to the ground on New Year's Eve 1936, and all the student and school board records burned with it. A new school, built of brick in 1938, now sits in the same location.

CHARLES BURNS SCHOOL: The school was built in 1914 and named after Burns, known as the first white settler in Big Bay. *Family photo.*

Powell Township Board meeting minutes from the beginning through the early 1930s show a pronounced emphasis on schools and roads. Charlie, who served both on the Board and the Highway Commission, was involved in much of the discussion, signing of petitions for new segments of roads to be built or bridges to be built and buttressed, and much more. Those records show the township allocated more than $100,000 in those early years for roadwork. It is not exactly clear how or when the new road was put through closer to its present location.

But in *The Story of Lake Independence*, Waring writes, "In 1910, when the Model T made its appearance in town, the trip to Marquette in the summer was only a four-hour experience instead of two days. However, if the gas gauge registered low, one had better back the car up the steep Sugar Loaf Hill so the gas tank, under the seat, could feed the engine. (It was fed by gravity.)"

Waring also goes on to say that the road wasn't plowed in winter until 1928.

GIRLS AT CHARLES BURNS SCHOOL, 1926
Front row from left: Eileen Reid, Algerna Aird, Helen
Clancy, Marion Swanson, Gladys Burns, Alice Thorpe,
Dorothea Wilson. Second row: Viola Burns, Lorraine
Gollickson, Jenny Burns, Florence Bonin, Ruth King,
Vernice French. Three girls on step behind second row:
Alice Prosen, Jean Hansen, Virginia Wheelock. On the back
step, just in front of back row: Erdine Lowe. Back row: K.
Aird, Gertrude Clancy, Dorothy Thompson, Pauline Laurich,
Tootsie Olson, Mildred Swanson, Jessie Lowe, Lois
Emmons. *Family photo.*

Charlie Burns remained involved with Powell Township, the
schools and roads, until he passed away in 1932. His obituary adds a
final exclamation point to his work.

"Charles A. Burns, Prominent in Life of Town, Died Yesterday,"
reads the headline of his obituary in the December 30, 1932, *Mining*

Journal. It goes on to say that he was the first white settler in Big Bay, and that he served as highway commissioner for more than thirty years. He also served on both the Powell Township Board and the PT School Board for several years.

From what is known and can be cobbled together, the elder LeClaires remained in their home on Burns Landing until they passed away. Jane died September 23, 1907, in Big Bay, and Morris died on March 13, 1916, in Big Bay. Jane LeClaire is buried in the cemetery at Assinins, but it isn't clear where Morris LeClaire is buried—his death certificate says Big Bay, but there is no burial record or marker at the cemetery there.

BOYS AT BURNS SCHOOL IN 1918: Standing, from left: Jack Ellsworth, Lyle Abrams, Milton Tompkins, Ace Whitney, Lloyd Moberg, Floyd Burke, Floyd Whitney. Seated, from left: Tom McGeorge, Peter Rasmussen, Chickadee Smith, Irish Caket, Bunny McDonald, Raymond Sharkey, Harry Hakala, Edward Sharkey. *Family photos*.

Charlie and Maggie continued to live at Burns Landing until they passed away. Charlie died December 29, 1932, and Maggie died about two weeks later, on January 12, 1933. Both are buried in the Big Bay cemetery.

Most of their children lived long lives, married, and had children of their own. However, two of their children died young. Margaret Bertha died on December 22, 1905 at nearly eighteen months of age. Eva Alice died on June 22, 1919 at nearly four years of age. She was tragically killed when a McGifford log loader ran over her near their home.

Two of Charlie and Maggie's sons who did not marry—Johnny and Victor—lived at Burns Landing until they passed away in 1968 and 1973, respectively.

Shortly after Victor died, Powell Township became the owner of Burns Landing. It turns out Charlie Burns sold the property to the Big Bay Lumber Company about six years after he purchased it, on January 19, 1903, retaining the right to use the buildings on the land until the new owner gave him one year's written notice to vacate. Burns Landing must have transferred to the Lake Independence Lumber Company, which purchased the mill. And it ended up with J. B. Deutsch, one of the owners who ran the mill and built the farm overlooking Burns Landing where Bay Cliff Health Camp now sits. Deutsch went into bankruptcy, according to Waring, and the mill returned to the Brunswick Company, which ran it until 1932. However, the Union National Bank ended up holding the property in Trust. The bank deeded the property to Bay Cliff Health Camp on March 22, 1938.

Then, on July 7, 1973—the year Victor died—Bay Cliff deeded the 3.85 acres Charlie Burns had owned to Powell Township for use as a public park. The township refurbished the original two-story log house, built a wooden pathway to the lake and a gazebo on the shore, installed restrooms, and overall created a lovely park now known as Burns Landing.

And so the Burns name lives on. Less known, or remembered, however, is the name of the original Native Americans who built there—Morris and Jane Mataxagay LeClaire.

Old Lady Lucy and Her Twenty-Five-Cent Moonshine

"Danny had been making moonshine and beer at Hungry Hollow long before an obscure politician called Volstead had leapt to a dreary sort of fame by vainly dreaming that he could impose sobriety on a restless nation by legislative fiat. The only noticeable effect Prohibition had ever had on the Hollow was to place a greater strain on the resources of Danny's battered still, and perhaps to make Danny more careful. 'They's more smellers and snoopers runnin' aroun' the woods these days than they's mosquitoes in our goddam swamp,' he had indignantly snorted."

— *Danny and the Boys* by Robert Traver (John Voelker)

ONE SUNNY AFTERNOON in the fall of 1966, my cousin Arline and I nervously parted the barbed-wire fence that separated the Big Bay Road from Old Lady Lucy's property. We gingerly crawled through and swiped a couple of apples from her prized trees.

Now, this story isn't so much about the theft, or the crisp, juicy apples that staved off our hangovers. It is about how terrified we were of Old Lady Lucy. Every kid who grew up around Big Bay from the

1920s through the 1960s was scared to death to go anywhere near her. She not only looked and talked tough, but she would chase you with a broom or shotgun if you dared set foot on her land. Kids whispered to one another what they had heard their parents say about her: Old Lady Lucy had killed a man inside her home that she had turned into a speakeasy during the Roaring Twenties. They claimed she had buried that man under the buckling hump that ran across the blacktopped road in front of her place.

Old Lady Lucy was a short, heavy woman with bushy, black intertwined eyebrows. Thick glasses rested atop her nose, and she almost always had a scarf wrapped around her head that was tied in a big knot at the top of her forehead. She wore those old-fashioned cotton housedresses that most women of that age wore, but she also pulled on a pair of long trousers underneath her dress. She rarely spoke to anyone. But when she did open her mouth to utter her usual "yep" or "nope" to a question, it was evident she didn't have many teeth.

Old Lady Lucy—she was never called anything but this by anyone in town—was married to a towering, 300-pound man named Art who always wore long-sleeved shirts and loose-fitting bib overalls. But by all accounts, she wore the pants in their family and ran everything, including their illicit business. And she fiercely protected what was theirs.

Gerald Beerman, Jr. lived with his grandparents in Hungry Hollow, just south of the Lucys. He told me over a cold one in the Lumberjack Tavern in the winter of 2013 that he remembered her well. "She was short and homely and really rough, manly. She didn't ask you to do something; she told you what to do and how and when to do it.

"Old Lady Lucy did all the talking and all the driving. Art didn't know how. And Art did exactly what she told him—and boy, he was after it," Gerry said with a mischievous giggle. The memories seemed to light him up as he vividly recalled stories from his childhood that colored in Old Lady Lucy's character.

The first had to do with her beautiful apples. "I remember Grandpa Beerman said he helped plant that orchard," Gerry said. "Old Lady Lucy ordered those trees from Montgomery Ward. Then she never made any payments on them. Monkey Ward wrote to her and demanded she either pay up or send the trees back. She wrote back and told them to come and dig them up if they wanted them."

Then Gerry, shaking his head and laughing out loud, remembered an incident with the Lucys' old "woody" station wagon. They drove down the steep, sand hill to Berklund's Sawmill on the west shores of Lake Independence to pick up free scraps of slab wood. "The old gal and Art loaded up the back of the car with the firewood," Gerry said. "But when Old Lady Lucy tried to pull out, the back wheels just spun in the sand. She turned to Art and told him to get out and pick up the ass end of the car and move it over, out of the sand. He did it too! Then she yelled, 'Set her down, Art, set her down.' And she gunned it and drove straight up the sand hill to the main road."

She was like a steamroller, Gerry said. Another time, Old Lady Lucy was stopped by the State Police as she was driving to Marquette. "The cops asked for her driver's license. She glared back at them and snapped, 'What's that? What's it for?' They told her that you needed a license to drive a car. And she said, 'Well, that's goddamned funny because I've been driving for forty-five years and ain't ever had no license.'"

The stories about the Lucys' more distant past are sketchy but consistent. The two came to Big Bay in the early 1920s—no one seems to know from where or how—but Art probably found a job at the town's main sawmill.

THE LUCY HOME, ORCHARD, AND "WOODY"
STATION WAGON: The Lucy's home, car, and orchard
are shown here in the spring of 1962; they are behind the
ruins of Temple's General Store, which had burned to the
ground. The apple trees, purchased from Montgomery Ward,
stretched from the front of their house to the Big Bay Road
Photo courtesy of Raymen P. Temple.

This was shortly after the end of World War I. Art had fought
and been wounded in the war. The shrapnel from a bomb remained
embedded in his back and caused him to be bent over and walk with
a limp for the remainder of his life.

This was also the era of Prohibition. Michigan passed a state
law banning liquor in May 1918; then the Eighteenth Amendment
to the US Constitution, called the Volstead Act for the Minnesota
Congressman who sponsored it, became law in January 1920. It
banned the production, transportation, and sale of alcoholic beverages
in the entire country, and remained in effect until December 1933.

But the Volstead Act had the opposite effect of what was sought
after by the temperance and religious leaders who fought for its
passage. It not only cost the government millions in lost tax revenue

on the sales of liquor, but it also cost the taxpayers many more millions in enforcement efforts because ordinary citizens refused to give up their drinking habits.

People all across the country began to brew their own alcoholic beverages in homemade stills, short for distiller—a contraption engineered to distill or produce wine, beer, and hard liquor. Some brewed alcoholic beverages for their own consumption, while others produced enough hooch to sell. As existing legal bars were forced to close, private citizens began to operate speakeasies, also known as blind pigs or gin joints, where customers could dance to live music, drink, and generally have a good time. By most accounts, there were as many as 100,000 of these establishments throughout the country.

Big Bay was no exception. Three to five speakeasies ran full-tilt at various times. And it had its share of stills, whose locations old-timers to this day are able to point out. For example, my mother's youngest sister, Mildred French Fleury, remembered the still her parents operated out back. "My mother made beer, and my father was known for his dandelion wine."

Big Bay, during the 1920s, was in the midst of one of its boom cycles. The Lake Independence Lumber Company purchased the sawmill in 1912 and ran it into the later 1920s. The owners spent more than $1 million rehabbing the mill and town, adding thirty new houses, as well as a new hotel, store, and boarding house. For several of those years, the mill operated two or three shifts a day. That sawmill was fed by timber from the surrounding area where at least a dozen logging camps, employing scores of lumberjacks, dotted the countryside. And as the lumber camp bosses ran pretty tight outfits with no alcohol allowed, these men were eager to travel to town on weekends in search of a good time.

Old Lady Lucy seemed to have the perfect spot for such a business—just south of Temple's General Store (now Cram's General

Store) on the outskirts of town. Art and she built a two-story house atop a small hill that was set back from the main road and tucked behind their apple orchard. Covered in a mock-brick-patterned, tan tarpaper, and completely wired for gas lamps before electricity arrived in the area, it was known as one of the nicest houses in Big Bay. It later became one of the first homes with electric lights and its own generator, as well as water pumped indoors.

As with most illegal businesses, official records are nonexistent. The Lucys, as far as anyone knows, never discussed their affairs or the troubles they encountered. But there are a few mentions of the business in newspaper stories as well as records that the courts retain.

Norman (Nummy) Boulden, a Big Bay old-timer, talked about the good times he and his pals had during Prohibition in a 1976 newspaper interview. He said on the weekends they would "sip moonshine at Old Lady Lucy's place hidden in the apple orchard, and dance until daybreak."

And *The Mining Journal* in 1984 printed an interview with Cora Beerman LaRouche, who moved to Big Bay in 1900 when she was two years old. Cora spoke with a reporter about the numbers of people who operated illegal stills and blind pigs in the Prohibition era of the 1920s. She said folks looked out for one another, though. The conductor of the train, which was the main means of transportation from Marquette to Big Bay at the time, would call ahead to the depot—home of the only telephone in town—to alert the locals if "revenuers," federal agents bent on busting those involved in selling liquor, were aboard the train.

The warnings helped the locals avoid several scrapes with the law. The Lucys, reportedly, would pull up a square section of floor that covered the stairs to their cellar and hurry their patrons down the steep steps. They would replace the cover and throw a rug over it before the revenuers showed up. That is supposedly how the one man got killed—Old Lady Lucy hurriedly pushed a throng of men down the steps, and, according to local lore, she pushed one a little too hard.

But the Lucys weren't able to escape the lawmen all of the time. In fact, a couple of ardent state troopers from Negaunee were most eager to put the Lucys—especially Old Lady Lucy—behind bars and eventually succeeded.

Art and Rose Anna Lucy were arrested for illegally possessing and selling intoxicating liquor (moonshine) at least five times between 1925 and 1929. Sometimes they escaped serious punishment, but as the revenuers revised and perfected their methods, the charges began to stick.

In an earlier arrest, the federal agents posed as lumberjacks, and in an attempt to fit in, they coerced a local young man, Johnny Burns, to visit the Lucy house with them at about seven-thirty on the evening of April 10, 1926. According to testimony given by law enforcement officers at a preliminary examination held in May 1926, Art Lucy greeted the men at the door and eventually admitted them to a front room. Art refused to serve them drinks inside the establishment, but he left them standing inside this room for a few minutes while he walked out behind the house to collect a pint of moonshine, which he sold them for $2.

Representing himself at this preliminary hearing, Art questioned the undercover state policeman who allegedly purchased the pint.

"What time was it about?" Art asked Fritz Enius, the officer.

"It was about seven-thirty Saturday night," Enius responded.

"I wasn't home that night," Art claimed.

Thomas Clancey, the prosecuting attorney, abruptly interrupted, and asked Art, "On April 10?"

"Yes," Art responded. "I wasn't home. I've got proof that I wasn't home at that time."

Mr. Lucy went on to say that at the time of day the officer claimed to have visited his house, it was dark outside, and there were no lights on inside his house because his wife was in bed with a headache.

The prosecutor addressed the state policeman again and asked if it was daylight or dark when he entered the Lucys' home.

"It was fairly dark," he answered. Enius went on to admit there were no lights on in the house.

Another officer, Charles Standish, who accompanied Enius, essentially provided the same testimony.

After Standish's testimony ended, Art Lucy said, "I think you are mistaken. You have better eyes than I have or anybody else around there. I have witnesses to that and I will fetch them up.... You fellows are framing up on me."

The court later dropped this case for lack of evidence. But the lawmen didn't give up. They harassed other locals, too, but none were charged nor harangued as much as the Lucys. The lawmen continued to send various agents in disguise and eventually obtained enough evidence to prosecute the Lucys.

Two different arrests resulted in $500 fines for Art and Rose Anna Lucy, which is equivalent to about $8,000 today. And both spent time—up to thirty days—in the Marquette County Jail.

But it is clear from the records that the officers wanted more. In 1928, the sting operations escalated, especially against Old Lady Lucy.

An undercover agent named Rollie Ramie was able to purchase whisky on five separate days in September 1928 from Old Lady Lucy.

Rose Anna Lucy appeared in the Marquette County Circuit Court on February 25, 1929, to face charges stemming from those sales to Ramie. She was convicted, fined $100, and sentenced to two years of probation. As part of the probation agreement, she promised to refrain from any illegal activities for the next two years.

For whatever reasons, Rose Anna Lucy did not keep her promise.

Only some three months into the probation period, at 11:40 a.m. on May 24, 1929, Old Lady Lucy entertained three guests in her dining room, serving them her homemade moonshine. One of them turned out to be a federal agent who, later that afternoon, appeared in the US District Court in Marquette. John G. Bednarz, an informant employed by the Michigan State Police, swore before the court that he had purchased three glasses of moonshine that morning from Rose Anna Lucy and paid her 25 cents for each glass.

Because of his testimony, the court issued a search warrant, which was executed by Ray Harring, Federal Prohibition Agent, at nine-thirty the next night. Mr. Harring listed the items he confiscated in a statement provided to the court: "1 syphon, 1 gallon moonshine, 2 pts beer, 1 part qt wine, 1 part pint moonshine."

Two days later, on May 27, 1929, the court issued an arrest warrant for Rose Anna Lucy. Shortly after, she was arrested and arraigned. The charges read in part: "in violation of the National Prohibition Act, [she] sold, possessed liquor and conducted a common nuisance."

The Mining Journal published news of the arrest on May 29, 1929, with a headline that proclaimed, "Hellhole of Big Bay Feels Sting of Law." It went on to discuss Lucy's arrest, as well as the arrests of five others, and said officers found at least a dozen "drunks" inside Lucy's house. The article went on to quote Haring, the federal agent: "We have done much to clean out a place I consider a hell hole…. I do not know a place in the Upper Peninsula in which the liquor situation has been worse than in Hungry Hollow."

Follow-up articles in *The Mining Journal* called Rose Anna Lucy the "Queen of Hungry Hollow," and called "Hungry Hollow the ill-famed paradise of lumberjacks on the outskirts of Big Bay."

The court ordered she pay $2,500 bail (about $41,000 today) to remain free while she waited for a grand jury to take up her case during the July term of the US District Court in Sault Ste. Marie, which is some 200 miles east of Big Bay. Because she couldn't come up with the cash, the court ordered she be taken to the Marquette County Jail and held until the July hearing.

She remained incarcerated at the Marquette jail, under Lord knows what conditions, from the end of May until mid-July.

Court records show that the evidence the court possessed—essentially the statements from Bednarz and Harring—was presented on July 6, 1929, to a Grand Jury seated by the US District Court in Sault Ste. Marie. That jury returned three counts against Rose Anna Lucy: two counts for the illegal sale of one glass of "moonshine whisky" that she had sold to Bednarz for 25 cents a glass in her dining room, and a third count for the small amount of liquor Harring later confiscated from their home, "moonshine whiskey, wine, and beer."

If there was a jury trial, there is no longer a record of it. All that exists is an indictment document signed by Fred M. Raymond, District Judge, on July 11, 1929:

> At a session of the District Court of the United States for the Western District of Michigan…in the US vs. Rose Anna Lucy that the defendant having been heretofore convicted and found guilty of the charges in said indictment contained, and being now brought into court and placed at the bar thereof, the Court now sentences her the said Rose Anna Lucy to be

imprisoned and kept at and in the Federal Industrial Institution for Women, at Alderson, West Virginia…for the period of three years.

The final two documents in the court record show that US Marshall Martin Brown delivered Rose Anna Lucy to the Federal Industrial Institution for Women at Alderson, West Virginia, on July 14, 1929, and that he received a receipt from the "keeper" of that institution confirming her arrival and imprisonment there.

That is the end of the official court record, and unfortunately, the women's prison at Alderson doesn't retain records after ten years. Nor are those records archived with the US government. It's, therefore, impossible to determine if Rose Anna Lucy served out the entire sentence—or how.

But Mrs. Lucy was most likely the first woman—and maybe the only—sent there from Upper Michigan. In fact, that women's prison, the first in the country, had only officially opened in 1928. Up to that time, women were housed with men in local jails often under appalling conditions.

Alderson, like Prohibition, was a new experiment in this country. In the early 1920s, in addition to prostitution and narcotics charges, more women faced Prohibition violations. Up to that time, they were tossed in jails along with men, and were reportedly subject to a litany of abuses. According to *The Washington Post*, nearly two dozen national women's organizations and the first female Assistant Attorney General, Mabel Walker Willebrandt, persuaded the federal government to construct a facility that would incarcerate women only and would try to rehabilitate, rather than punish, them.

The West Virginia property was chosen because it was close enough to Washington, DC—a five-hour drive today—and in an area so isolated that escape would be difficult. It officially opened in 1928 and housed 200 female prisoners at the time. It eventually leveled off at about 500 prisoners—long after Old Lady Lucy was incarcerated there. And it has been the prison home to several infamous women, including the World War II propagandist "Tokyo Rose," jazz legend Billie Holliday, Charles Manson follower Lynette "Squeakie" Fromme, and more recently, Martha Stewart.

UNITED STATES OF AMERICA

WESTERN DISTRICT OF MICHIGAN

SOUTHERN DIVISION } ss.:

I do hereby certify and return that, in compliance with the terms of the within Sentence, I have delivered the within-named ______ Rose Anna Lucy ______ to the __ Keeper ______ of the Federal Industrial Institution for Women at __ Alderson, West Vir. __, in the county of ______, and State of Michigan [Ohio], on this __ July 14, __ day of ______, 192 9, and have taken the receipt of said __ Keeper ______ therefor, which is attached hereto.

Martin Brown
____
U. S. Marshal.

By______________________
Deputy U. S. Marshal.

INCARCERATION DOCUMENTS: Rose Anna Lucy receives three-year sentence, essentially for selling three 25-cent glasses of moonshine. A US Marshal then delivers her to the first women's penitentiary in this country at Alderson, West Virginia.

District Court of the United States of America

WESTERN DISTRICT OF MICHIGAN

SOUTHERN DIVISION

At a session of the District Court of the United States for the Western District of Michigan, continued and held in the City of _______ Sault Ste. Marie _______, on the ___ 11th ___ day of _______ July _______, in the year of our Lord one thousand nine hundred and _______ twenty-nine _______, and of the Independence of the United States the one hundred and ___ fifty-fourth. ___

Present, the Honorable _______ Fred M. Raymond _______, District Judge.

Among the proceedings then and there had were the following:

UNITED STATES	No. __2717__
vs.	Indictment ____________
Rose Anna Lucy	Viol. Nat. Pro. Act.
	Sales.

The defendant having been heretofore convicted and found guilty of the charges in said indictment continued, and being now brought into Court and placed at the bar thereof, the Court now sentence ___ her ___ the said _______ Rose Anna Lucy _______ to be imprisoned in the _Federal Industrial Institution for Women, at Alderson_, in the County of ________________ and State of _______ West Virginia _______, subject to the rules and regulations of that institution, for and during the term and period of _three years_, from and including the ___ 11th ___ day of _______ July _______, A. D. 192 9.

I, _______ Orrie J. Sluiter _______, clerk of said Court, do hereby certify the above and aforesaid to be a true copy of the sentence of said Court upon _Rose Anna Lucy_ so entered in the records of said Court on the day and year above written.

WITNESS my official signature and the seal of said Court at Grand Rapids, this ___ 12th ___ day of _______ July _______, in the year of our Lord one thousand nine hundred and _______ twenty-nine _______

____
Clerk.

It must've been a long ride for Rose Anna Lucy to the hills of West Virginia—close to 1,000 miles. There's no way of knowing what she thought of the facility located on 200 acres in the foothills of the Allegheny Mountains, or of the rehabilitation programs it offered.

But she must've been housed with a dozen other women in one of sixteen two-story cottages that were situated on a college-like campus. A documentary on the facility says that newer arrivals were placed with longer-serving inmates who could teach them how to get along there. The female prisoners were assigned one of several jobs: the facility had electric sewing machines with which the prisoners made all their uniforms, bed linens, tablecloths, and drapes for the windows. Other prisoners tended extensive gardens, where they grew much of their own produce. Others operated small equipment in their own dairy farm. And others cooked and served all the meals.

PRISON COTTAGES: The south fronts and east sides of the lower quadrangle of cottages are shown in this photo of The Federal Industrial Institution for Women in Alderson, West Virginia. *Photo courtesy of Library of Congress.*

After serving her time at Alderson, Rose Anna Lucy returned to Big Bay. It's difficult to know how the prison experience affected her. But it had to have had an impact, considering how far away it was from her home, her husband, and her only daughter, who was a teenager when Rose Anna Lucy was sent away.

With hindsight, it is much easier to see how she may have become bitter not only by her incarceration, but because her peers in the area had been treated differently—no one else from Big Bay went to a federal penitentiary. And others with more resources who flouted the law went unscathed.

For example, just a few miles down the road from the Lucys, in what could be more aptly described as a world away, was the site of Granot Loma.

"It was the magnificent summer home of Louis and Marie Kaufman," writes Russell M. Magnaghi in his book about the era, *Prohibition in the Upper Peninsula: Booze & Bootleggers on the Border*. "Louis was an extremely successful Marquette and New York banker, who, among his many accomplishments, put together the financial packages that created General Motors and financed the Empire State Building."

Magnaghi goes on to explain how Kaufman built the largest Adirondack-style log cabin in the world on his Lake Superior property and was savvy enough to include "two huge side-by-side bank vaults whose massive steel doors were marked 'his' and 'hers.'" Kaufman, Magnaghi writes, had purchased the entire contents of a liquor store in Manhattan that had been forced to close because of Prohibition. Kaufman shipped that liquor by rail to Granot Loma.

"During the 1920s and 1930s, this stash of booze was used for parties they hosted for the rich and famous, who arrived by Kaufman's private rail car. Houseguests came from Hollywood to New York and included Fred Astaire, Mary Pickford, Lionel Barrymore," among others. "Far from prying eyes, his guests could enjoy his magnificent estate and hospitality."

Moreover, about the time Old Lady Lucy was most likely released from Alderson, Prohibition came to an end. The public, and therefore the politicians, became disillusioned with its consequences and considered it a failed experiment.

"An Association Against the Prohibition Amendment pamphlet claimed that between 1920 and 1931, $11 billion was lost in federal liquor tax revenues while $310 million was spent on enforcement," Magnaghi writes.

Moreover, he goes on to say, "The Anti-Saloon League promoted the idea in 1916 that prohibition would totally eliminate prisons. Instead, there was talk of adding new ones at taxpayers' expense. The governor of Michigan had to parole four hundred liquor violators to make room for future convicted violators."

Then, in a further affront to Old Lady Lucy, Ray Harring, the Federal Prohibition Agent who built the last case against her, lasted only thirteen months on the job. "[H]is failure to pass the Civil Service examination caused him to resign in the spring of 1930," Magnaghi writes.

Those circumstances might go a long way in explaining why the Lucys became so reclusive and apparently never let anyone inside their house again. For the remainder of their lives, they tended a large garden on their property as well as the magnificent apple orchard, and they raised hogs.

Tom Abbott, eighty-eight, of Big Bay, told me in the fall of 2021 that when he was a kid, he would go up behind the Lucys' house with his dad to help butcher the hogs in the fall. The Lucys would give them a hog for their help. But, Tom says, he was never allowed inside the house.

That's the way they kept it until they passed away. Rose Anna Lucy died on March 26, 1963. Art, more crippled than ever, accepted a little help afterward. But as far as anyone knows, no one visited inside the house.

Raymen P. (Tuffer) Temple, whose dad owned the store next to the Lucys' property, brought Art his newspaper every day after Mrs. Lucy died, and checked to see if he needed anything from the store. Art would sit at the kitchen table, just inside the back door that had a glass window in the top half.

"He'd come to the door and would have me put my hand out, and he'd squeeze this little leather coin purse into my hand so I'd get some change.

"One day I went over, he wasn't sitting there. I opened the door and hollered. Nothing. So I ran back to the store and got my dad. We couldn't find him in the house. So we went out back to the outhouse. He was sitting on the shitter, stiff."

That was July 15, 1963. Today, the Lucys' house has been razed. The hill on which it stood, including the bountiful apple orchard that surrounded it, has been plowed under, flattened, to make room for a legal business.

The Civilian Conservation Corps Arrives in Big Bay

O NE DAY IN the mid-fifties, my younger sister and I were stuck inside, bored, because of a raging snowstorm. To entertain us, my mother let us climb the ladder to the attic to dig through her family treasures stored in the old, beaten-up trunk that had belonged to her father. We found school papers and drawings belonging to my oldest brother, who had died from polio at age eight in 1940. We discovered paper dolls and a cloth doll my mother played with as a child. We found postcards my mother received as a baby in 1909 and 1910 from my great-grandmothers. And we found a pair of dark khaki, wool breeches that had belonged to my father.

We giggled at the bloused-out hips on the pants, and the long laces at the tightly-fitted lower sides of the legs. We didn't know what breeches were or how they had been used, only that they had been part of my dad's CCC uniform and that we weren't allowed to play with them. That is my first memory of hearing about the presence of the Civilian Conservation Corps in Big Bay, Michigan.

Little did I know those breeches had been leftovers from World War I. And I certainly didn't know how this program had helped so many young men and their families through the desperate times of the Great Depression and also created profound, lasting environmental benefits.

WORLD WAR I SWAG: Claude Bowers, author's father,
shown here in 1935 in his CCC-issued uniform.
The clothing the CCC enrollees received was surplus from
World War I. *Family photo.*

The latter part of the 1920s and early 1930s was the worst time my parents and others of their generation experienced. Nearly half the country's banks failed in the aftermath of the 1929 stock market crash, and more than 15 million people lost their jobs.

"It is hard to forget being 'laid off,' having no work or income," writes John O. Simonds, one of the fortunate young men to secure a slot with the CCC in Big Bay. "It is hard to forget doctors cutting fireplace wood and selling it house to house.... Or unemployed architects selling vegetables on the street. Hunger pangs are common."

The government stepped in to help with a massive relief and regeneration program known as the New Deal. Its architect, President Franklin D. Roosevelt, presented an emergency act to Congress that would create the Civilian Conservation Corps shortly after he was inaugurated on March 27, 1933.

The CCC would provide manual labor for unemployed young men aged 17-25. These men would be paid one-sixth of a salary and the remaining five-sixths of the salary would be sent to their families. At the same time, the work they performed would also benefit and conserve the country's national resources. The emergency act was approved by Congress within four days, and by April 17, the first CCC camp, run by the US Army and US Forestry Service together, officially opened. By July 1, nearly 275,000 young men were put to work. Eventually, some 5 million young men enrolled in some 2,900 camps across the country from 1933-1942. Close to 30,000 young men from the UP eventually enrolled—about 10 percent of the UP's population.

"By early 1933," writes Larry Chabot in his comprehensive book about the CCC in the Upper Peninsula of Michigan, *Saving Our Sons*, the unemployment rate in the UP was "35 percent—ten points above the national average." He goes on to write that, "By early 1934, 45 percent of Upper Peninsula residents—143,345 people— were on welfare," the highest per capita welfare cost in the country.

Big Bay did not escape the maelstrom. The Brunswick Lumber Company, which at the time operated the sawmill in Big Bay and owned the town as well as the surrounding lumber camps and timberland, shut down in May 1932 because of the Depression. This meant the houses in the village of Big Bay would no longer benefit from the electricity generated by the mill or water that was pumped from the mill up the hill to the town's houses. Even the town doctor, who had been employed by the mill, left.

"There was no market for the lumber…. There was no employment in the town after that for four years," writes Betty A. Waring in *Yellow Dog Tales and Logging Trails*. She goes on to say that "Many houses were sold by the company and moved away, and the town was reduced to half of what it" had been.

That explains why so many people of my parents' generation spoke so reverently of the impact both President Roosevelt and the CCC had on Big Bay.

The first mention of Camp Big Bay, one of 120 CCC camps located in the Upper Peninsula, came in the fall of 1933. *The Mining Journal* published an article in October that reported, "Camp Champion… in Marquette County is to be known in the future as Camp Big Bay and is to be moved to a new site three miles southeast of Big Bay on County Road 550." The young men who were to be encamped at Camp Big Bay, also known as Camp 690, would work on fire access roads, telephone lines, dams, and fisheries projects on inland lakes, the article states.

It was to be a cooperative effort between the federal and state governments. The 3627th Company of the US Army would provide military leaders to run the camp, with the same military-style structure and discipline administered at US Army bases. At the same time, staffers from the US and State Forestry Services would choose the projects to be completed and lead the work crews. Those projects would entail heavy work: restoration of spent national resources. But the military structure, discipline, and education would help the young men to grow up and become responsible, self-reliant, and productive members of society. Around 200 men, up to 250 at its peak, served at a time in Camp Big Bay. A few of them came from Big Bay and other towns in the UP, while most came from Lower Michigan, especially the Detroit area.

OFFICERS AT CAMP BIG BAY: US Army officers and
state forestry service personnel collaborated to establish
military-style order while forestry projects were completed.
US Government photo.

Orval Nicholson was one of the earlier enrollees, who enlisted
for the typical six-month stay but was allowed to re-up at the end of
the enlistment period. He was only sixteen at the time, but like many
of the men, he fibbed about his age to get in before his seventeenth
birthday. When Nicholson arrived in Big Bay by train from Ann
Arbor in April of 1934, snow still covered the ground. "They were
building the barracks. The only thing here was a supply tent and a
building to eat in. We stayed in tents," he told John Underhill in a
1985 interview.

Camp Big Bay was situated on a piece of cutover, basically
barren land a little south of Alder Creek. When completed, there was
a gatehouse, five wood-framed barracks, a cook house, a mess hall, a
recreation room, a water tower, a library with books and magazines

CAMP BIG BAY: The buildings that housed the CCC
enrollees; the materials to build them were salvaged from an
abandoned Army training post.
US Government photo.

where educational classes also were held, and equipment sheds. The
structures were covered with tar paper and lathe and were roofed
with corrugated metal. The materials for these buildings had been
salvaged from an abandoned Army training post.

As the young men arrived, they were issued Army supplies
left over from World War I: uniforms that consisted of jackets and
breeches, like the ones I found in the trunk, work clothes, shoes, a
hat, gloves, coats, towels, toilet kit—everything an Army enlistee
would receive.

"We got…underwear, shoes, socks, shirts, four pairs of pants,"
Mr. Nicholson said. "When anything got worn out, you just went
over to the supply sergeant and got replacements."

The young men earned $30 per month; $5 they kept and $25 was
sent home to their families, which basically doubled the amount of
money the families had received on welfare. Towns like Big Bay
began to recover as these operations grew. Lumber and carpenters
were required to build the camps, and myriad supplies were needed
to keep them running. Plus, the young men's families now had cash

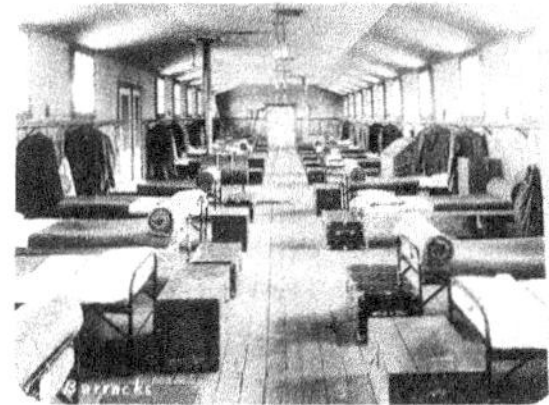

COMFORTS OF CAMP: Shown here, a bunk room, the mess hall, and the rec room. *US Government photo.*

to purchase not only food, but shoes, clothing, and other household goods.

A typical day for the men at Camp Big Bay began at 6 a.m. when Reveille played over a loudspeaker to awaken and summon them to roll call and morning exercises. Breakfast was served promptly at 7 a.m. and consisted of a basic feast for men who had known real hunger: bacon, ham, sausages, eggs, potatoes, hotcakes, fruits, and bread, according to John O. Simonds, who wrote a memoir about his experience at Camp Big Bay. Then the leadership handed out work assignments to the young men and loaded them in trucks to ferry them to their work project locations. They would work until noon when the Camp cooks would deliver lunch to the men. After lunch, the laborers returned to their jobs until 4 p.m., when they piled into trucks to return to Camp Big Bay for supper.

Simonds says, "one could expect fish, fowl, and meat in some form. Always with hot breads and pastries. Each night a different pudding and flavor of freshly churned ice cream."

Afterwards, the men had free time to visit the recreation hall, or participate in classes or sporting activities. The men began taking showers at 9:30 p.m. and prepared to turn in. Curfew and lights out was 10 p.m.

The CCC in Michigan planted more trees than any other state, some 485,000,000 trees in total.

Peter Raymen French, a Big Bay native who served with the CCC in Manistique, was interviewed by John Underhill in 1985. French remembered a phrase taught him during his service. "If we are to pass on to our posterity the natural resources as they've been passed on to us, it is going to be necessary to alter the present-day policy of ruthlessly destroying the forests."

Although the CCC planted some trees around Big Bay, it wasn't a priority because trees weren't needed. The pines there hadn't been completely clear cut as they had in the rest of the state.

Camp Big Bay had three main goals: the eradication of "blister rust" disease—a fungus that spread through gooseberry bushes that attacked and killed the pines; the prevention of forest fires, a major threat to the area's economy and natural environment; and fish habitat improvement.

State forestry officers trained the Camp workers so they completely understood the blister rust disease, how it manifested, and how to clear the gooseberry bushes that served as hosts for the fungi. Eventually, the Camp Big Bay crews cleared the host bushes on 31,293 acres of land around Big Bay.

The second area of concentration, and arguably as important, was work to prevent and fight forest fires, thereby protecting the standing timber—the continuing source of local revenue. Fires had proved disastrous in the past, partially because it was so difficult to travel through dense forests to fight the blazes.

Fires, whether set off by loggers and their equipment or lightning, proved disastrous all over the state in the early 1900s, with hundreds of thousands of acres having burned. The Big Bay area was no exception. In 1922, a fire that started in slashings, the leftovers of logged land, spread from Birch toward Big Bay and burned nearly 2,000 acres of timberlands. In 1923, a fire southwest of Big Bay started on the railroad tracks near a logging camp where eighty men

BUILDING ROADS: Here, CCC enlistees work on one of
the several access roads they built during the early 1930s.
Photo courtesy of The Marquette Regional History Center.

worked. The fire blazed through 1,200 acres and trapped five
lumberjacks, who lost their lives and are buried in graves with only
white crosses, no names, in the Big Bay cemetery.

To provide better access to the backwoods, the Camp Big Bay crews cleared the brush along miles of roadsides and built additional roads to gain easier access to fires. Many are still used today for access and recreational activities. Among them: Sullivan Creek Truck Trail, Mulligan Creek Road, Alder Creek Truck Trail, Bushey Creek Truck Trail, Wilson Creek Truck Trail, and the Triple A Road.

"The most common method of fire-fighting is to get well out ahead of the blaze with a wide enough cut to break the wall of flame," Simonds writes. "My job was to clear the line with an axe and grubhoe, then drive stakes at 100-foot intervals as guides to the grading equipment and crew to follow. We did this under foreman Morse who had laid out fire trails all his life and who was constantly appraising the problems, possibilities, and alternatives."

Simonds goes on to say, in his memoir about his experience at Camp Big Bay, that each member of the CCC "worked under an experienced foreman…. The work was tough and new to each crew member, but they soon learned to handle at least a small part of the operation well. Once a farmhand or even a city street punk learned to sight a transit, or wield a trowel, or fell a tree without 'hanging it up,' there was a growing sense of pride in accomplishment."

These crews also constructed fire towers that were manned for decades with fire spotters. They built the Hairpin Curve Tower on old M-35 by the Hairpin Curve and the Panorama Tower, a 100-foot structure just south of the Triple A and Ford Road intersection that looked out over Big Bay, the Huron Mountains, and Skanee.

"The boys at the Big Bay Camp take much pride in their jobs and do not wait for the foreman to arrive and give the duty signal," said E. G. Amos, administrative officer for the US Forest Service. He stopped to inspect the work on the new towers while vacationing in the area. An article in *The Mining Journal*, dated August 24, 1935, tells about his visit. "Stripped to their waists, and chests out, these young men scale the towers 'like a bunch of monkeys' and throw bolts and wrenches back and forth with the greatest of ease like trained steel workers,' Mr. Amos said.

"They were singing 'Home on the Range,' when I arrived, and it was such an inspiring sight that I forgot about taking a vacation," Amos went on to say. "The public hears a lot about what the forests are doing for the CCC, but a lot of people are still too ignorant about what the CCC are doing for the forests," he said. He invited the public to tour the camps and see firsthand what the crews had accomplished.

The third priority for Camp Big Bay was to improve the fish habitat. "The first crew I was assigned to was the river rat crew," Bernard Bridges, a former Camp Big Bay enrollee, told John Underhill in 1985. "We removed beaver dams and other obstructions."

"Youths in the CCC Camp in Big Bay…placed 600 fish shelters in Lake Independence," a May 17, 1935, article in *The Mining Journal* stated. "They set 60 fish shelters, spawning beds, and minnow beds in Saux Head Lake, their lake improvement work involving 4,420 acres."

To build the fish shelters, the CCC crews gathered the brush they cleared from the roadsides. After the lake froze in the winter, they piled the brush up and weighed down the corners. When the ice melted in the spring, the shelters sank to the bottom of the lake.

In addition, they mapped the bottoms of both Lake Independence and Saux Head Lake. They repaired the cement dam where Lake Independence flows into the Iron River and added a fish ladder.

In addition to the workday, the men were provided continuing education classes. One of the vehicles for furthering the young men's education classes was a newsletter, written and published by the men at Camp Big Bay.

The young men wrote newsy items, as well as reports on their extracurricular exploits, in their newsletter, called *The Kodak*. The Marquette Regional History Center has a copy of the May 1935 issue, which highlighted educational opportunities available to the enrollees:

> LARGE NUMBER ENROLLED IN NEW CLASSES. Four new educational classes have been started recently with seemingly a great amount of interest, judging from the number of men who have enrolled. The new subjects consist of: Auto Mechanics by R. Carrier; Blue Print Reading by F. Masek; Radio by E. Neilsen; Cooking by J. Mandley.

My dad was likely in that auto mechanics class that continued throughout the year. He enlisted on September 1, 1935, and served at the Big Bay Camp until June 10, 1936, according to his military records. By that time, the CCC had extended its criteria to include both older and married men. My dad would have been thirty-three, married, and the father of two sons at the time.

My brother Bert, now eighty-eight, remembers Dad's uniform, the heavy jacket, breeches, and high-top boots. "When Dad came home from work, he'd sit in a chair and let me and Claudie [my brother who died from polio in 1940] pull off those high boots."

Mr. Danford Emblad, Chief Foreman at Camp Big Bay, critiqued my father's skills and performance: "Ability as a workman: Very Good. Special Qualifications: Roadworker, Mechanic at Whse #2, Tractor Driver."

My two older brothers, as well as other old-timers, herald my dad's mechanical skills. He performed repairs on all his vehicles, taught both my older brothers to do the same, and helped many friends with their cars.

The newsletter also shows the young men not only learned to tell good stories, but they also had some fun with their language skills.

GRANDSTANDING: Claude Bowers, left, unknown
civilian soldier, and Leonard Wicketts watch a baseball
game at Camp Big Bay in 1935. *Family photo.*

In the May 1935 issue of The Kodak, the boys published an
"Official Announcement" that read:

> At this time, we take very great pleasure in reserving a
> small portion of our paper for an announcement which we
> know will interest and excite each and every one of us. The
> rumors of the past about the camp's moving have become

an established fact. We are going to move, and it will be in the northeast corner of Isle Royale to a place called Utopia. Only a quarter of a mile from camp is a girls' school with an age limit of 18 to 21 years. At the present time there are 200 pupils attending the school. A few hundred feet to the west of camp is a large beer garden which has a capacity of approximately 400 people and beer sells for 10 cents a quart. A large bathing beach is near at hand. Just think of it fellows. Just think of IT!

The newsletter covered their recreational activities with a "Sport Flashes" column on page 15:

Flash-On May 27, the hardball team went to Skandia and won by a score of 9-3. The prospects of this year's team are very bright. L. Wicketts was picked by his teammates as the most valuable player. He is also outstanding in his batting, besides being the camp's pitcher.

"Wicketts informs the writer that he believes Dizzy Dean has nothing on him. He concedes that Rube Waddell was just a little better—because he was a left-hander. That is why Wicketts is carrying gasoline cans with his left arm. Trying to develop the old flicker, eh?"

They had more good times than with just the paper. The young men had evenings and weekends mainly to themselves. The Army provided equipment for baseball, basketball, soccer, and other games. In addition, the recreation hall was furnished with pool and ping pong tables. And the local establishments, with Prohibition ending in 1933, now provided both liquor and entertainment on the weekends.

Norman (Nummie) Boulden worked his way up to sergeant in the Big Bay Camp, and he was assigned to look after the young men on weekends, as well as in the woods, he said in a 1976 interview with *The Mining Journal*.

PLAYING TRUCKS: Morris Tinkham, an enrollee at
Camp Big Bay, runs his toy truck through the snow behind
the real Camp Big Bay Truck.
Family photo.

"In a town that boasted only 15 girls to 150 men, lumberjacks and CCC boys fought for a female partner, then learned to dance without one. If there weren't enough girls to go around, there were fights for everyone."

They often went to Joe Borro's dance hall in Hungry Hollow. "Jim Cherrette played violin, accompanied by his wife at the piano, and Charlie Vande Zande on the drums. They played until midnight for $10 and $1.50 per hour after that."

"One night when the fighting got heavy," Boulden said, "I backed a truck to the door, lowered the tailgate and threw in everyone wearing a CCC uniform." When he got back to the Camp, he says, he found two strangers in the tangle and one man from Big Bay.

To avoid those establishments, Boulden decided to hold a dance in the mess hall at the Camp and invited girls from both Big Bay and Marquette. He said the weather was quite humid, and shortly after the girls arrived, the floor became sticky, so he sent one of the boys to the kitchen for cornmeal to scatter around. "The kid got mixed up, grabbed the wrong box and dumped 10 pounds of oatmeal" on the floor, which created quite a "gummy mess."

Those "mixed up" kids also had a soft side. One evening in 1935, as the men returned from a day of work in the woods and began to clean and store their tools, someone let out a shout, writes Simonds. "There, staggering into camp was a wounded fawn—shot high in the front leg, with hide hanging bloody and loose. She collapsed as we gathered around and sent for the visiting Doc."

The doctor cleaned the wound, sewed the torn hide back in place, and bandaged the leg. A man who oversaw the tool shed broke open a bale of hay to make a bed for her at the back of the small building. "That was her home from then on," Simonds writes. "He'd lock her in at night to protect her from dogs or a possible bear. In the mornings, he would let her out. Soon she learned to streak for the cookhouse door where she knew would be waiting a fresh loaf of cornbread set out with a half bucket of milk."

FAWN FINDS HOME: Russell Carrier entertains a fawn at Camp Big Bay. *Family photo.*

By 1937, a new World War loomed and the country began to change. "Unemployment had dropped to 14.3 percent, a cut of almost one-third from three years earlier…cuts were on the horizon," writes Larry Chabot in *Saving Our Sons: How the Civilian Conservation Corps Rescued a Generation of Upper Michigan Men.*

Indeed. Camp Big Bay closed in May 1937, with the remaining enrollees transferred to other camps still operating. The program was phased out completely in 1942 following the December 7, 1941, bombing of Pearl Harbor when the United States quickly switched to a war footing. Many of the enrollees, in fact, transferred into military service.

Simonds, who earned degrees from Michigan State and Harvard and went on to become a prominent modern landscape architect, ends his *Recollections of Life in the Big Bay, Michigan, Camp of the Civilian Conservation Corps*, with a chapter called "Leaving." It consists of one sentence. "Leaving the Big Bay CCC camp after a year, for an opportunity to continue my schooling, was one of the saddest days of my life."

It seems many of the men who served at Camp Big Bay talked about the benefits of their CCC service for the rest of their lives. It basically saved their families and taught them work skills and ethics to help them in any career path they chose.

In the summer of 1995, some of the men who had served in Camp Big Bay returned to place a plaque at the site where Camp Big Bay once stood.

Ben Mukkala wrote about the small reunion in the September 17, 1995, issue of *The Mining Journal*. He asked the men who showed up what they thought of their experience. Most told him how proud they were that they were able to help their families at the time with the money the CCC sent to them, and that the skills and ethics they learned carried them through their lives.

A. J. "Swede" Anderson, who was originally from Skanee, had joined up in Ironwood, and traveled from there by train to Big Bay, told Mukkala he had recently retired as woodlands superintendent for the American Corporation and said his time at Camp Big Bay was "19 fun months that started my career in the woods."

Gerry McGlue, who also attended the reunion, was born in

L'Anse but had spent four years at the orphanage in Marquette. He missed his train to Big Bay when he was supposed to report and had to walk all the way— some thirty miles. But of his enrollment, he said, "I think it was the cat's meow."

Romeo Carafelly, from Detroit, said he was fed only one or two meals a day there. At Camp Big Bay, he was fed three good meals a day and given a good start in life. "Everything was beautiful," he told Mukkala.

Albin Zigila said he was walking the streets of Detroit in really bad shape until he joined the CCC when he was only sixteen, another enrollee who fibbed about his age so he could get in. "I could have been in jail," Al told Mukkala, shaking his head. "Instead, we learned the work ethic."

My dad, who passed away in 1970, never forgot what the CCC did for him and his family. He was also a lifelong fan of President Roosevelt and the Detroit Tigers and never could shoot a deer.

RIGHT—CAMP BIG BAY
ENROLLEES: Photo of all
enrollees during 1935 taken by a
US government photographer.
US Government photo.

From Big Bay to Detroit: 1947 Class Trip

AT EIGHT O'CLOCK sharp on the morning of June 25, 1947, sixteen freshly scrubbed, anxious students showed up at the school in Big Bay. They didn't get up early to attend summer school or to take more silly tests. Instead, they intended to climb aboard their school's bus for the biggest adventure of their young lives and one that would provide them with an educational experience they couldn't learn from books. It was to be a class trip to Detroit for eighth-grade graduates, a practice that became a tradition.

Joseph Strieleman, Principal of Powell Township School, sat behind the steering wheel of the Ford bus, which had recently been painted, red, white, and blue at one of Henry Ford's plants in the Upper Peninsula. Stella Rymkos, teacher, joined the group as a chaperone for the long trip to Detroit.

It's well known that Henry Ford, early in the twentieth century, forever changed the economic landscape of this nation with the introduction of his affordable, assembly-line produced Model T. Much less known about the man, however, is the enduring impact he had on the lives of many young people he came in contact with while engaging in various business interests in small towns such as Big Bay.

Two of those youngsters, Albert (Bert) Bowers and Kathryn (Kitty) Spehar L'Huillier, when in their mid-eighties, shared memories from their childhoods of when Ford purchased the sawmill and most of the small town of Big Bay, Michigan. The highlight, for them, was their 1947 class trip. But they also recall how Mr. Ford befriended the local kids, tossing them a quarter to buy ice cream. Ford also paid for extracurricular activities at school, and even aided several young people in town who suffered from various afflictions.

Ford long had ties to the area. In 1929, he became a member of the Huron Mountain Club, a sprawling, private pleasure club for wealthy people located on the shores of Lake Superior in a remote part of the Upper Peninsula, near Big Bay.

When Big Bay's original school, a wood-framed structure named after early pioneer Charles Burns, burned down on December 31, 1936, members of the Huron Mountain Club pitched in to rebuild a new school, now a brick edifice. In addition, Ford himself donated one of his new buses to transport students from rural areas into town.

Then, in August 1943, Henry Ford purchased the then-idle sawmill and most of the declining village of Big Bay. He immediately rehabilitated the mill, complete with a new power plant that also supplied the town. He developed a new water-supply system for both the mill and town, built The Big Bay Hotel from a dilapidated company store, and restored many of the town's company houses that had fallen into disrepair.

"It gave us new impetus to go ahead," Mr. Strieleman said in a 1951 interview for Ford Motor Company. "And it looked as if we could really look forward to something, which we did."

Mr. Ford held many business meetings in the lobby of the hotel he had built, which is located directly across the street from the school and was later named the Thunder Bay Inn.

"We always played on the porch of the hotel," Kitty says. "Henry Ford would come up from the water—he had some kind of plane that landed on Lake Independence—and shook hands with all of us, and gave us money for ice cream."

Ford played a bigger, behind-the-scenes role as well. In 1944, when Bert and Kitty were sixth-graders, the sawmill—now up and running—invited the sixth, seventh, and eighth graders to tour the facility, with an assignment attached. The children were to take notes and write an essay to explain how the mill operated. The student who wrote the best essay in each of the three grades was awarded a prize from Ford: a $25 war bond.

"I won the contest in sixth grade," Bert says, still beaming.

Ford also paid outside professionals to teach the children in the upper grades of the school to dance.

SCHOOL PHOTO: Bert's eighth grade photo from Powell Township School. *Family photo.*

"We followed Benjamin Lovett's book and his customs," Strieleman said. "The Ford Motor Company paid the piano players to come in and furnish the music for all this."

Both Bert and Kitty fondly recall the dance classes. "Juanita Clarke played the piano and her husband Charlie taught us how to dance," says Kitty. "Those classes were a huge hit with the students, and to this day most of us can cut a rug."

The two also remember a playmate who suffered from severe, involuntary muscle spasms. Mr. Ford saw young Fannie Jacobs playing in the street and decided to help. He moved her to the Ford Hospital in Detroit, where she was diagnosed with St. Vitus Dance. Ford moved her family there as well, providing them with a house and a job for the girl's father at Greenfield Village. Moreover, Ford regularly visited the children at Bay Cliff Health Camp—a summer camp that hosts handicapped children—and paid for treatments for them that sometimes stretched to at least a year at the Ford Hospital in Detroit.

DANCE INSTRUCTORS: Charlie and Juanita Clarke on the shore of Lake Superior, 1940. They later taught PTS students to square dance and waltz.
Photo courtesy of Linda Miles VanDamme.

But the most memorable gift, according to these students, was the school trip that followed their graduation from eighth grade in 1947. Most of these kids had never been out of Big Bay, let alone visited a big city.

The student group included: Sharon Bingeman, Bert Bowers, Ray Bowers, Diana Britton, Eileen Fraley, Virginia Koziol, James (Jitny) Narovitch, Carol (Pavie) Rasmussen, Kitty Spehar, Wayne Stroh, Dewey Thorpe, Charles (Bud) Temple, and Mary Vardon—all eighth-grade graduates. In addition, three students who graduated twelfth grade in Marquette but were from Big Bay were invited to join them: Robert (Bobbie) Rasmussen, William (Billie) Edwards, and William (Bud) Hutter.

According to Strieleman, he and Gerald Wolfe, superintendent of the Ford plant in Big Bay, conceived the idea with "educational and recreational" elements for the students. The children had to raise the money to pay for their travel expenses to and from Detroit. Ford agreed to cover the hotel and activities in Detroit.

Bert and Kitty say their mothers helped with bake sales, community dances, and lunches. In addition, Mr. Strieleman helped the students obtain and sell commercially produced ballpoint pens, which were fairly new. They earned enough money to pay their railway fare, as well as to pay for most of their meals.

Mr. Strieleman drove the bus eastward, across the UP to St. Ignace, on the north side of the Straits of Mackinac. It was already early afternoon, but they had to wait to catch the next ferry across the Straits (yes before the bridge) to Mackinaw City on the northern tip of the Lower Peninsula. To pass some time, they visited Castle Rock—a nearly 200-foot high column of limestone, shaped like a castle, that overlooks the north side of the Straits.

CASTLE ROCK: The 1947 graduates from Big Bay stopped to see this 200-foot deposit truf limestone near St. Ignace while waiting for a ferry to cross to the Lower Peninsula of Michigan.
Photo courtesy of Library of Congress.

Late that afternoon, after the close to one-hour ferry crossing, and a short walk to the train station, the jolly group boarded Michigan Central's Northerner for Detroit.

The next morning, Carmie Frazzini, one of Ford's most trusted drivers, met the students from Big Bay at the twenty-one-story Michigan Central Depot in downtown Detroit. Mr. Frazzini would chauffeur the group in a Ford bus around the Detroit area for the next five days. First stop: the Detroit Leland Hotel, a majestic, Italian Renaissance structure situated downtown on the corner of Cass and Bagley Avenues. Skyscrapers towered all around them.

LELAND HOTEL: The towering hotel, with crank-operated elevators, was home to the Big Bay students for nearly a week. *Postcards (above and on page 106) courtesy of Boston Public Library.*

Bert and Kitty say they, and the other students who had never been beyond Marquette, were dazzled by both the exteriors and interiors of these buildings. Bert shared a room on the twenty-third floor with his cousin, Bud Temple. It was their first elevator ride, and Bert says that the boys, especially, were awestruck by the crank-operated elevators, not to mention the young women who operated them. He says, "When they flipped the crank, you went up or down really fast. We road up and down and up and down," he says with a giggle.

The next several days were so jam-packed with activities that it has become a blur, both Bert and Kitty say. Their driver, Carmie, picked them up early each morning for scheduled visits. They toured The Henry Ford Museum and Greenfield Village, visited the famed Ford Rotunda for lunch, and dined at the Dearborn Inn that evening. "We had to wear suits and dresses, hats and gloves, and it was the first time we saw cloth napkins and real silver," Kitty recalls.

They toured the River Rouge auto plant, where they walked the entire assembly line. They spent one day at Eastwood Park—a large amusement park on 8 Mile Road and Gratiot that operated from 1928 to 1952. They visited a zoo on Belle Isle, took a short trip into Canada, and the grand finale—a double-header at Briggs Stadium on Sunday, June 29. The Tigers were finishing off a five-game series against the St. Louis Browns (the Tigers won all five).

"The one thing I remember about the baseball game is they had this popular player—Hoot Evers," Bert says. "He got up to bat, and I had turned to talk to somebody next to me and heard this loud crack. It sounded like the bat hitting a ball, but the ball had hit Evers in the head. Everybody started yelling—when I looked down, he was lying flat out on the ground at the plate."

According to an article in the online database *Society for American Baseball Research*, "On June 29, in a game at Detroit, pitcher Bob Muncrief of the St. Louis Browns hit Evers in the left temple and he was taken to the hospital." He did recover and returned to the team twelve days later.

HAMMING IT UP AT EASTWOOD PARK: Students pose in a fake jail cell. LEFT—Front from left: Stella Rymkos, teacher and chaperone, Diana Britton, Carol (Pavie) Rasmussen. Back from left: Ray (Bud) Bowers, Mary Vardon, William (Bud) Hutter, and Bud Temple. RIGHT—Front from left: Sharon Bingman, Katharine Spehar. Back from left: Bob Rasmussen, Bud Hutter.
Photos courtesy of Katharine Spehar L'Huillier.

In addition to the supervised activities, these young students slipped out of their hotel for a couple of clandestine outings. One night, Kitty and her three roommates snuck out of the hotel to visit a nearby drugstore "that carried everything under the sun." One other night, several of the students snuck out to a theater to see an adult-rated movie, *The Outlaw*, starring Jane Russell. "The theater was real ritzy," Bert says. Indeed, the United Artists Theater at 150 Bagley Street was one of the downtown Detroit theaters whose "intricate designs and lavish interiors…became as much of a draw as the movies themselves," states the website historicdetroit.org.

One of the favorite and enduring memories of this group—in addition to all they experienced—is that eighth-grade graduate Mary Vardon and twelfth-grade graduate Bobbie Rasmussen "hooked up on that trip, and they are still married to each other to this day," says Bert.

Those memories and that marriage survived, as did the tradition started in 1947 for class trips for the eighth-grade graduates of Powell Township School. However, after Henry Ford died and the mill in Big Bay closed, the school lost that financial support for the trips. The school shifted focus in the early 1950s, creating fundraisers to pay all the expenses, as well as changing the destination to the nation's capital. The trips now take place every other year so seventh and eighth graders are included on each trip. "That means more people to raise money and a longer time to do it," says Linda Fleury, who retired in 2014, after teaching at PTS and leading class trips for forty-one years.

What began as a one-week trip to the state's capital has morphed into a one-week trip to this nation's capital, or to both New York City and Washington, DC. But the residents of Big Bay to this day embrace the tradition started in 1947.

Big Bay, Beyond, and Back

Pete Raymen climbed into his new, shiny black Model T Ford and left the little lakeside town of Big Bay, Michigan, at daybreak on Thursday, the 21st of June in 1923. He stopped in Marquette for gas, which set him back a buck-eighteen, and then struck out for Alaska—the last frontier to men of his age.

It was the grandest adventure and greatest challenge that Great-Uncle Pete undertook. For the first time in his life, he shook off the familial obligations he had shouldered since childhood. Approaching midlife, he unabashedly embraced the romantic tug of the road leading West, as had so many before him. But he was also part of a new wave of early twentieth-century pioneers who helped build the backbone of the United States—those who made it possible for this country's Henry Fords to develop and open the economy to middle Americans.

A heat wave had enveloped the entire Midwest that first official week of summer in 1923, and it was already nearly ninety degrees. So, Pete, a handsome, forty-five-year-old redhead with light blue eyes, snapped down the top half of his windshield so the breeze wafting over Lake Superior cooled his face. He headed south toward Escanaba on what was then known as M-15. He set the pace of his touring car at about 20-25 miles per hour and reached a tourist park in Rapid River in time to fix his dinner—bacon fried over an open fire, and stuffed into his mother's homemade buns that he'd brought from home.

Pete had prepared well for this arduous, cross-country trip, something akin to crossing the Atlantic in a kayak today. He carefully packed the Model T with assorted tools, camping equipment, and his shoelace-strapped scrapbook of maps and miscellaneous information he'd need to transport him through his 3,000-mile journey, with a planned stop in Montana for a Fourth of July World Heavyweight Boxing Championship between Jack Dempsey and Tommy Gibbons. He strapped two additional five-gallon cans of gasoline to the running boards, along with jugs of drinking water. He also carried with him an ample supply of self-confidence, a marriage of raw curiosity, and successful work experiences that seamlessly melded with the economic boom of the post-World War I 1920s.

It was the age of possibility in the United States. Anyone, it seemed, could become an overnight millionaire. Common people challenged conventions like never before, pushing boundaries. Besides affordable cars, radios were introduced to the masses. It was the age of Prohibition, speakeasies, jazz, and the new, modish young women known as flappers, who wore daring, briefer styles and swaddled themselves in fox fur. That created the demand for increasingly valuable fox pelts—the prices had tripled to $130 each by 1920, up from $47 at the onset of World War I—and provided the motivation for Pete's current entrepreneurial pursuit.

The entire economy was heating up. Pete saw a report in *The Mining Journal* that claimed the economy was growing at 5 percent annually, and that unemployment was at 0 percent because of the demand for "skilled labor of all kinds."

Moreover, US President Warren G. Harding had set out on a cross-country train trip, which included several whistlestops for speeches

FORD MODEL T: The restored 1923 Model T touring car pictured here is similar to the car Pete Raymen drove from Big Bay to Seattle in 1923. *Author photo.*

as well as a ferry ride from Seattle to Alaska, three days before Pete began his journey. The president's aim: to open the Alaska Territory to more trade.

After Pete ate, he packed up the few items he'd removed from his Model T and motored on into northern Wisconsin. At day's end, he stopped at a wooded tourist park on Pelican Lake near Antigo, where he spent his first night under the stars. He unfurled his large frame from the front seat, and, ever frugal, carefully unpacked his fishing rod and a small tin of night crawlers covered with damp earth. He cast his line into the lake and caught a mess of yellow perch, which he fried in his black cast iron skillet over an open fire. Before he turned in for the night, he noted in his journal, which I acquired about two decades ago, that his speedometer read 113 miles when he left Big

Bay early that morning and now registered 348 miles. His journal is written on expense-book paper in his barely legible, cryptic cursive. It includes the highlights of Pete's days, what he paid for food, gas, and other supplies, the mileage recorded by the Model T, and brief descriptions of problems he encountered.

Pete certainly didn't possess the polish of an East Coast MBA; nor did he hold a blue-blood pedigree. Approaching forty-six years of age, Pete was a six-foot-three-inch outdoorsy guy, much more skilled with wrenches than silverware.

The second child and first son of eight children, Pete was born on September 5, 1877, in the dusty railroad siding of Blendon, in Ottawa County, Michigan, on what is now the campus of Grand Valley State College. Pete's father, Jacob Einsiedler, a German immigrant, was already forty-four years old and scarred from fighting in the Civil War when Pete was born. His mother, Sarah Jane Fonger, was twenty-four years old. She had been born to German-English immigrants in the same county in which she gave birth to her eldest children. A first-generation American, Sarah was well educated for the period and insisted on the same for her children. When Pete turned six, his mother sent him and his older sister to the nearby Blendon School District No. 1, a one-room, bare-bones schoolhouse where one young teacher taught grades 1-8 the basics: reading, writing, arithmetic, geography, and history.

RAYMEN FAMILY c. 1891: Sitting from left: Peter F.; Jacob, holding May; Ray; Sarah Jane, holding Florence; and Letty. Standing from left: Edith, Frankie, and Louella. *Family photo.*

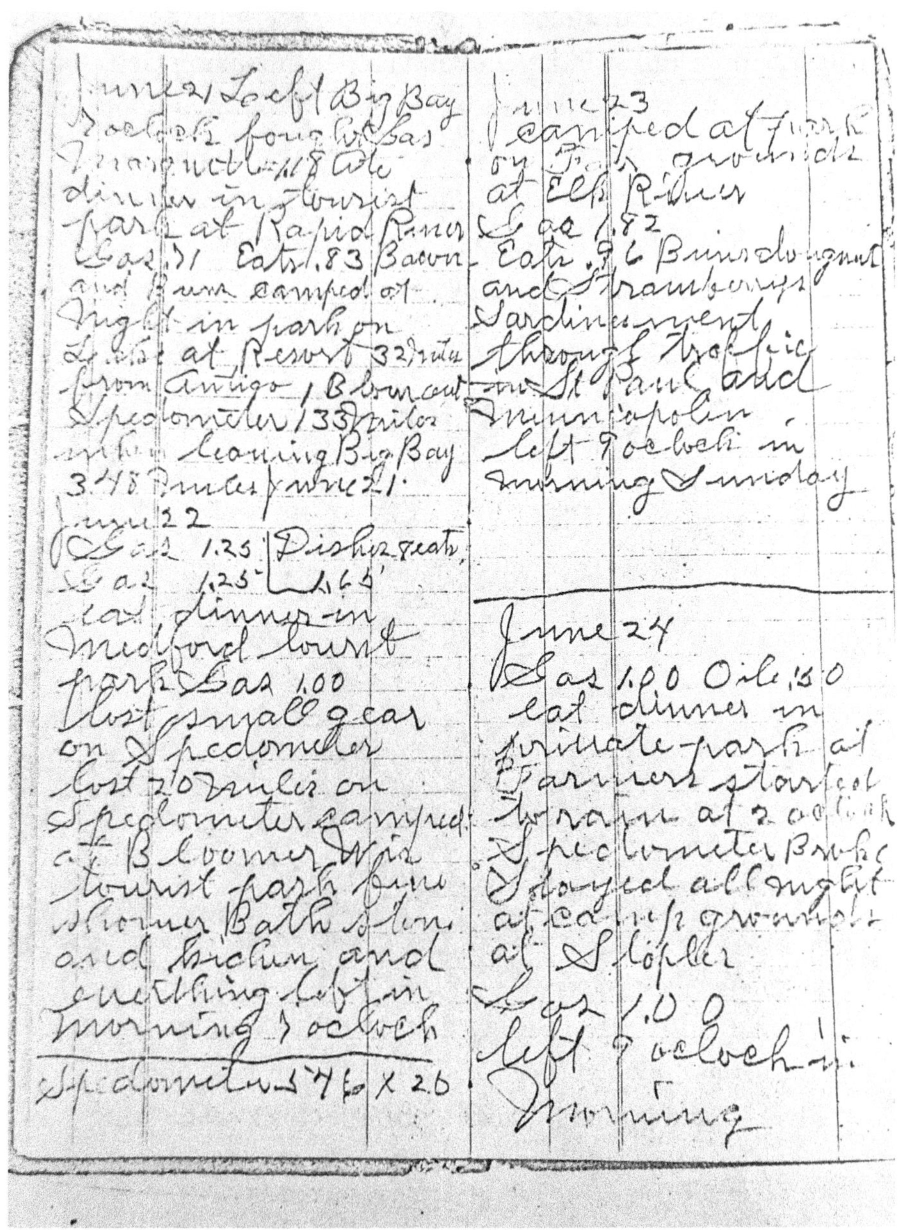

BARE ESSENTIALS: Pete wrote sparingly about his days in his journal, pictured here. *Author photo.*

Pete's education, however, was abruptly interrupted during his third-grade year when his family desperately needed his help.

Jacob's health had declined from wounds and illnesses inflicted during lengthy Civil War marches and battles, including Gettysburg, and he had become too frail to work alone. From that point, Pete, now nine years old, went to work every day with his father, gradually assuming his father's responsibilities. He learned to skid logs from the woods, load them on wagons, and drive them with teams of horses from the forests to a nearby sawmill.

RAYMEN FAMILY: Sitting from left: Edith, Letty, Jacob Sebastian Raymen (nee Einsiedler), Sarah Jane Fonger, Peter F., and Frankie. Standing from left: Florence, May, Louella, and Ray. About 1905. *Family photo.*

By the time Pete turned sixteen, he had effectively become the patriarch of the family, which had adopted the Americanized surname "Raymen," supporting his parents and younger brother and sisters. He also had become a sawyer in the mill where he'd worked. My grandmother, May Raymen French, Pete's younger sister, frequently and proudly proclaimed, "You know, my brother Pete had his own sawmill by the time he turned sixteen."

Pete did have his own small mill that he'd cobbled together from scrap parts, where he tinkered in his spare time, honing his skills. But he continued to hire out for bigger logging companies. He maintained all the running machinery in the mills where he worked. He also disassembled the mills when it was time to quit one location and then reassembled them at new sites, following the lumber camps of men carving their way through the grand forests of central and northern Michigan and then up into the Upper Peninsula. Four of his sisters and their spouses, along with his one brother, and later his mother, followed him and remained near to him for the remainder of their lives.

Pete also continued to tinker, to try to develop his own industries. When The Northern Lumber Company, which Pete worked for in 1912, moved its operations from Birch—another, now disappeared, logging town about halfway between Marquette and Big Bay—Pete reclaimed some abandoned machinery and a vacant building. There, he created his first commercial operation—a cross-country ski and snowshoe factory, where he put members of his growing family to work for a short time.

RAYMEN BROTHERS: Ray, left, and Pete, probably mulling over one of their business endeavors. *Family photo.*

Mildred French Fleury, who was born in 1921 and was Pete's youngest niece, recalls that when she traveled from Big Bay to Marquette to attend high school, classmates raved to her about skis they'd purchased from Uncle Pete.

Millie also recalled the large role Pete played in their upbringing. She said Pete spent a great deal of time coaching his siblings' children—the nephews, especially—as they grew up in Big Bay in the late 1920s. There were three boys about the same age: Peter Raymen French, John Raymen, and Harold Mitchell. Two of them, French and Mitchell, tragically lost their fathers when they were quite young. Pete schooled these boys on how to shoot a gun so they could provide meat for their families, coached them in the art of brook trout fishing, taught them to drive his car, and even showed them how to build a house. But probably most important, Pete built a small-scale clothespin factory on the back forty to provide practical training for the boys in machine shop skills. (All three nephews went on to work in machine shops.)

"I swear, those boys thought he was a god," Millie said. "On Saturday nights, when those three boys were about sixteen, Pete would let them take turns using his car. He'd fill up the tank with gas and give the boy five dollars to take his girl out."

But it wasn't only family members who placed Pete in such high regard. Nearly everyone in town, older family members and friends recall, turned to Pete when they needed to know how to repair a car or a piece of machinery, wanted advice on how to land a job, or sought to uncover some arcane fact. "Let's ask Pete," was a common refrain.

Even Henry Ford drove up to Pete's clothespin factory one day seeking a favor. Mr. Ford began to frequent Big Bay in the early 1920s to visit The Huron Mountain Club, a private pleasure club for wealthy Americans along the shores of Lake Superior. Later, in the

HENRY FORD: Ford, so the family story goes, drove up
to Pete's clothespin factory to persuade him to come out of
retirement and return to work for him.
Family photo.

1940s, he purchased the defunct sawmill in Big Bay as he continued
to expand his auto-manufacturing business. As the story goes,
according to two nephews who were present, Ford said there was
no other millwright as good as Pete, a man who could "walk into a
factory, listen to the equipment hum along, and know within three
minutes which piece of machinery had malfunctioned and how to
fix it." Pete did agree to leave retired life behind and work for Ford.
Indeed, for a total of twelve years, Pete served as superintendent of
maintenance at four of Ford's Upper Peninsula plants.

But it was Pete's trip to Alaska that was the most meaningful and
daring—and inspiring—of his personal business ventures.

Pete had an insatiable curiosity, and read voraciously—Marquette's daily, *The Mining Journal*, and several magazines, including *The Saturday Evening Post*, *Collier's*, and *The Fur Trade Journal*. He clipped and made notes about items that piqued his interest, such as the news about the upcoming World Heavyweight boxing match promoted by the small town of Shelby, Montana, and the uptick in prices for fox pelts. With both, he saw an opportunity to increase his knowledge of business operations and set up a fox farm that would put his growing extended family on a firm financial foundation. He seized the prospect without reservation, as he had every other opportunity he had tackled earlier in his life.

To set up his new fox ranch, Pete wanted the best stock available. Those turned out to be blue foxes, and he had to travel to Alaska to procure them. Over the dark winter months of 1922-23, Pete plotted out his trip and knew he would need his mechanical acumen and all the moxie he could muster to accomplish his mission.

It was still a full three decades before President Dwight D. Eisenhower began to champion an interstate highway system and a full six decades before that network was completed. There were no decent road maps, or a chain of motels where one could place advance reservations, or regularly spaced service stations, or even a radio in the car for company. But all that was part of the appeal to Pete—rare, solitary time to think, plus all the more of a challenge for him to conquer.

Five days into his journey, after some 600 bumpy miles and hours of whistling all the tunes he could remember, it "rained the hardest I ever saw; knocked down all the corn and grain alongside the roads," Pete wrote. "And I could not get over the bad roads without chains, and then the speedometer began to run backward."

Pete pulled out his blanket roll, tools, and cooking utensils the night of June 25, 1923, at Casselton, North Dakota, just west of

Fargo, and began to repair the Model T before dark. He detached the speedometer cable from the left front wheel, where it was incorrectly fastened, causing the speedometer to run backward— perhaps when he changed a flat tire. Then he reattached it to the right front wheel, which correctly engaged the speedometer to record forward-moving mileage. This speedometer fix was vital for his trip; the directions in the *Automobile Blue Book* from 1920 are provided in mileage, e.g., at 3.9 miles from Marquette, "Right-hand road, store on right; turn right. Avoid right-hand road 4.6. Pass Yalmer P. O. on left 12.5."

Route 330—Marquette to Escanaba, Mich.—79.2 m.

Reverse Route 307.

Via Chatham and Trenary. Gravel and stone roads to Trenary; balance macadam and dirt.

Route 329 offers an excellent option via Carlshend.

Route 329 to Carlshend, combined with Note (a) on Route 329 to Little Lake, and Route 331 to Escanaba offers an option via Little Lake and Lathrop.

For this and other exits see **City Map**, page 276.

—MILEAGE— Total Mileage	Distance Between Points	
0.0	0.0	**MARQUETTE,** Washington & Front Sts., banks on left. Go south with trolley on Front St.
0.2	0.2	4-corners at RR; turn left onto Baraga St. and at far side of park, turn right onto Lake St. Cross RRs 0.4-0.7-0.8-0.9. Cross RR 2.1, avoiding right-hand road just beyond. Cross RRs 2.4-3.1.
3.9	3.7	Right-hand road, store on right; turn right. Avoid right-hand road 4.6. Pass **Yalmer P. O.** on left 12.5.
14.4	10.5	Left-hand diagonal road; bear left. Keep right thru diagonal 4-corners just beyond, passing wooden store on left.

MAP OF THE TIMES: Pete followed directions like these,
from the *Automobile Blue Book*, throughout his journey
from Big Bay to Seattle.

Before his crossing concluded, Pete would have to make several, crucial repairs to his car along the lonely roads. He patched countless flat tires; replaced the generator; routinely cleaned out the carburetor, coils, and spark plugs; and replaced gaskets and the fan belt several times.

His notes are curt and dry, and slightly humorous, which, according to accounts of several people who knew him, was quintessential Pete.

After he fixed the speedometer problem that Monday evening, Pete built a campfire and began to prepare his evening meal—bacon and buns. Suddenly, he noticed he was no longer alone, and this really irritated him: "This tourist park is no good," he writes in his journal. "There is a driveway in a circle around the park, and all the nuts keep coming around looking at you as if they had a private zoo. And no one has come to camp yet but myself."

Pete resented the intruders for looking at him as if he were an exotic animal, but also because they interrupted the peace he cherished; not even the countless hours of driving alone balanced out the time he had spent taking care of others and their problems. He loved the uninterrupted time to plan the remainder of this grand adventure, to consider the inducement of the Alaska territory, as well as to plot out the necessary steps to set up his fox farm. He also appreciated the quiet, natural world around him, where he was most comfortable. He loved to listen to coyotes and wolves howl at night, to spy a deer or moose in a distant meadow, or to amble to a nearby stream, where he would drop a line and hook to catch dinner. And he loved nothing more than taking apart and putting back together his cars—these machines were his personal playgrounds.

Pete's first car was, by all accounts, his "love child," only the second-known car to travel the road from Marquette to Big Bay. He purchased it soon after the first car arrived in Big Bay, owned by J. B. Deutsch, the man who owned the Lake Independence Lumber Company, where Pete worked at the time as a millwright.

May French, my grandmother and Pete's younger sister, recalled that Pete pulled into her driveway with this new car—something that must have looked like a spaceship landing today. "He said, 'C'mon, May; let me take you for a ride.'" My grandmother said she told him in no uncertain terms she wasn't climbing inside his latest contraption. She recalled that Pete was absolutely driven to try out any and all newfangled creations he could find—from hunting traps to shotguns to vehicles. He also had the first radio in Big Bay, she said. That radio, purchased mail order from Montgomery Ward, also was tucked inside Pete's Model T for company during the long winter that faced him in the Alaska territory.

After twelve days of jolting over 1,543 miles of mainly rugged roads in ninety-degree temperatures, a sweat- and dust-crusted Pete Raymen rolled into Shelby, Montana, at 9:30 a.m. on July 2, 1923. He found a space to park his car and pitched his tent in a tourist park that had been haphazardly set up next to the train tracks for the thousands of "motor tourists" expected for the Fourth of July World Heavyweight Boxing Championship.

Pete wrote in his journal that the camp was little more than a patch of prairie grass, but it had "good gas burners to cook on and running water." He bathed in one of the new "shower baths," dressed in his suit and ever-present fedora, and set out on foot to explore the area and learn what he could about the upcoming fight.

Situated in a bowl inside a barren circle of low-lying knolls, Shelby was laid out east to west along the Great Northern Railway tracks that ran through town. For the boxing match extravaganza, the company had added a second, parallel set of tracks, where the Pullman Company parked a line of sleepers to accommodate the more than 100 newspapermen covering the event and other expected guests. The depot, a long, narrow, board-sided building, had been doubled in size. The Great Northern Company had promised the fight's promoters that it would add at least twenty-six trains from the East and West Coasts in the few days before the fight.

Pete headed toward the downtown area on Main Street, which like all roads leading into Shelby, was dirt mixed with a little gravel.

A banner stretched above the street greeted visitors: "Shelby, the Oil City." Model T Fords, clones of Pete's, as well as wagons pulled by horses, lined the streets. Behind them, businesses flourished. The population, according to town officials, had grown from about 500 in January of 1923 to some 6,000 by early June.

The clapboard-sided storefronts included, among others, Benjamin's General Store, Larson's Shoe Store, the Park Hotel, the Silver Grill, the Red Dog Saloon, Aunt Kate's Cathouse (not a pet shop), and the King Tut dance hall. Midway up the street stood the newly constructed Chamber of Commerce building. It contained offices for the newspaper people, plus a public telephone and telegraph service, and it served as the center for information about the upcoming fight.

On the far western edge of town, on the south side of the Great Northern's tracks, stood the new arena, an impressive behemoth. Built to seat 40,000 people from 1,250,000 board feet of yellow pine timber that had to be hauled into this treeless country, it covered a full twenty acres.

Several tents had been planted around the arena where hot dog and soft drink vendors had set up business. In the distance, on the low-lying hills, a number of Blackfeet Indians had pitched their teepees. They had traveled from their nearby reservation to take part in what they called a stampede—another word for a rodeo—prior to the fight.

It was a lot to take in for a conservative, unsophisticated man like Pete, who had never seen a crowd, let alone these other fascinating attractions that previously he'd only read about. Local ranchers sported ten-gallon hats, boots with spurs, and six-shooters slung low on their hips. Professional cowboys—even the movie star Tom Mix on his horse Tony—in all their get-up had traveled to Shelby to take part in the Wild West show. Members of the Blackfeet Indian

Nation expertly sat astride their horses in the streets, bare-chested in headdresses and leather leggings. All sorts of side businesses had sprung up: hotels, dance halls with orchestras imported from Minneapolis and Seattle, bootleggers—this was also the era of Prohibition. Large tents housed a myriad of concessionaires, and several tents staged traveling plays. Women sported riding trousers, not yet seen in the East, let alone Pete's hometown of Big Bay. Airplanes, which must have seemed otherworldly, flew overhead nearly continuously.

Pete made his way back to the Chamber of Commerce building. Reporters and tourists alike awaited news. The excitement was palpable—would there be a fight, or would there not?

That was a question Pete had read about continuously since late February of 1923, when he first saw the news about the possibility of the July 4 World Championship boxing match.

He had read in *The Mining Journal* that Jack Dempsey, the renowned World Heavyweight Boxing Champion for the past four years, had agreed to fight the little-known Minnesotan Tommy Gibbons, in—of all places—the tiny prairie town of Shelby, Montana, located only fifteen miles from the Canadian border.

Pete was astonished. He had been following Dempsey's prizefights in his local newspaper, as well as on his new Montgomery Ward radio, and even in moving pictures of live matches that were occasionally shown at the Delft Theatre in Marquette. Dempsey had defended his title only two times in the past four years. That a match of this magnitude was being scheduled now and might be staged along the route that Pete intended to travel on his way to Alaska seemed almost too fortuitous.

Pete was interested in boxing and followed it, as he did all the major trends. But he was more fascinated by the big business side of the venture than the so-called sport of men brutally beating one another. The amounts of money being bandied about seemed almost ludicrous—Dempsey was to receive a record $300,000 for showing up to fight, which would compute to about $5,000,000 today. Montana's financial promoters of the bout expected to rake in as much as $1.5 million ($20 million today) for staging the match.

But this was, after all, the Roaring Twenties. Following the defeat of Germany in World War I, America breathlessly rushed toward a brighter future. "Ownership of cars, new household appliances, and housing was spread widely through the population," economist Gene Smiley, an emeritus professor at Marquette University, wrote on EH.net. "Like the Internet boom of the late 1990s, the electricity boom of the 1920s fed a rapid expansion of the stock market."

Pete definitely wanted his slice of this economic pie. He had fought and scratched his whole life to achieve success. Excelling and mastering every task placed before him, he reckoned, would prepare him to move up the proverbial labor ladder of success. He was ambitious, curious, and clever—he carefully watched and learned from the people who had achieved the level of success he sought. He patterned his attempts after the best he could, from the millwrights he first worked for to his favorite businessman, Henry Ford—the man who made automobiles affordable for the ordinary American, and made himself staggeringly rich in the process.

Now, these men in Montana he'd been reading about had an extremely aggressive get-rich scheme. And, it seemed, they'd met their match in Jack Dempsey's crafty manager, Jack Kearns.

From what Pete had read about the man, Kearns was a self-educated, street-wise, and extremely cunning businessman who had earned a reputation for his shrewd business transactions. He had been born in Michigan, like Pete, but spent most of his younger life in Seattle. Kearns had gone to work at a young age, as Pete had, and was even more adventurous. At age fourteen, Kearns had stowed away on a freighter bound for Alaska. Gold was his pursuit. But instead of striking it rich in an underground mine, he found running gambling schemes on the streets nearly as lucrative. Kearns made enough money to comfortably return to Seattle, in style, he wrote in his autobiography. He went on to smuggle undocumented Chinese immigrants into the US—rowing them ashore from ships anchored four miles off the Seattle Coast. He started his own newspaper, played semi-pro baseball, and eventually became a boxer himself before becoming a manager for other, more famous pugilists. He never stopped looking for the next gold rush, any business scheme that presented a pathway to a bigger triumph.

Pete was driven in much the same way, albeit on a smaller scale. He constantly looked for the next big idea and hatched ideas to build a business that would fill a specific, local niche.

In those short, dark days of February 1923, when Pete first read about the boxing match, he also read about President Harding's plans to promote more trade with the Alaska Territory during his upcoming trip. And he read about the demand for fox pelts and began to devise his own scheme.

Pete carefully designed his business plan, which would include a cross-country trip to Alaska to procure the foxes to bring back to Big Bay, where his younger brother would help him with pens, breeding, and selling the furs. As he calculated the costs and benefits of his plan, he became more interested in the schemers in Montana and their dealings with the wily Jack Kearns.

According to a published account, several ranchers, oil speculators, and real estate moguls sat around a small office in February 1923, boots on desks, brainstorming how they might lure settlers from the East to their dusty frontier town. An oil field had recently been discovered near the town, and these men wanted to exploit it. James W. (Body) Johnson, one of the youngest men present, had seen a newspaper item in *The Great Falls Tribune* that day that piqued his interest. The item said the city of Montreal had offered Dempsey $100,000 to fight there. The son of Shelby Mayor James A. Johnson, Sr., one of the wealthiest ranchers in the state and owner of half the businesses in Shelby, Body Johnson suggested they up the ante and offer Dempsey $200,000 to fight in Shelby.

These businessmen thought if they could entice Dempsey to fight in Shelby, they could attract—first and foremost—the national press corps to publicize the match. While the newspapermen covered the match, the businessmen's thinking went, they would naturally also want to write about the area's newly discovered oil fields. Then, masses of people, as in the 1849 California Gold Rush, would flock into the area to develop this barren flatland located fifteen miles south of the Canadian border.

The businessmen fired off a telegram to Dempsey's manager in New York, Jack Kearns, offering the World Champion $200,000 if he would fight in Shelby on July 4, 1923. Within a few days, Kearns responded: "Ready to do business immediately provided you have your representative meet me here prepared to pay me $50,000 and post another $50,000 as forfeit upon signing articles."

"You could have bowled me over with a feather," Body Johnson wrote in the July 4, 1968, issue of *Sports Illustrated*. "I decided to make the most of it and drag it out as long as possible. I called the local Helena reporters and Associated Press representatives… and gave them the story and content of the telegrams of offer and acceptance, and this really did make the headlines."

"The whole thing started as a gag, then developed into a good publicity stunt, then into a financial nightmare," Johnson wrote. Johnson's first task was to bring on board his friends at the local American Legion Post. Montana had only recently legalized boxing with the caveat that—as in much of the rest of the country—the profits from the matches go to veterans' groups. Loy J. Molumby, a Great Falls attorney and State Commander of the American Legion Post, agreed to help. An early May meeting was then set up to solidify the business deal at a Chicago hotel.

Molumby, representing the Montana investors' group; Kearns, representing Dempsey; and Ed Kane, manager for Tommy Gibbons, convened on May 4 at Chicago's Morrison Hotel—a modern high-rise for the times, the only hotel outside of New York City to reach more than forty floors. The three men, as well as the hotelier, tell similar but differing accounts of how the deal went down. What seemed clear, after the spilled beer congealed and the blue smoke haze lifted, was that Molumby and Kane were greatly outgunned by Kearns, who was rail-thin and almost always dressed up in multi-hued pastel—often pink—silk shirts, ties, and suits along with a straw boater hat.

Kearns, who was an excellent manager of press coverage because of his newspaper experience, put on an elaborate bash for the men. They reportedly drank and gambled into the wee hours of the morning. What emerged, besides bedraggled men, was a signed document that changed the course of the boxing match. The fee due the Dempsey/Kearns team increased from $200,000 to $300,000. Because Kearns prematurely leaked the increased amount of the fee to his reporter friends, the news played across the front pages of the nation's newspapers the next day.

"In complete disregard of our instructions, Loy Molumby agreed to the fateful, and, for us, disastrous contract in a smoke-filled room of the Morrison Hotel," writes Johnson, who was in the hospital recovering from an auto accident at the time. "I shall never forget that morning…when nurses brought in *The Great Falls Tribune* with the headlines: Managers Agree To Hold Title Bout At Shelby. The story went on to say that the championship fight would be held in

Shelby, Montana, on July 4, 1923, the consideration to Dempsey to be $300,000, $100,000 in cash at the time of the signing of the contract, $100,000 to be paid on June 15, and $100,000 to be paid on July 2.”

Johnson, who had written a personal check for the first installment, and his cronies not only had to come up with two additional $100,000 cash installments, but they also had to build an arena to seat 40,000 spectators, as well as hotels and camping areas to house them, and restaurants and concessions to feed them; to pipe in enough water to quench their thirst; and to create side events to entertain them. These monumental tasks played on the front and editorial pages of the nation’s papers, including Pete’s local daily.

An editorial in the May 6, 1923, issue of *The Mining Journal* opined on the monumental task Shelby faced, saying the cost of production of the match would easily exceed the outlandish amounts paid the fighters. “Only Western nerve would chance it,” it ended.

The nation’s papers continued to speculate about the upcoming match as Shelby’s businessmen struggled to come up with the cash for the second two payments to Kearns, as well as the $75,000 to pay for the new arena. With both Shelby’s businessmen and Kearns feeding them tidbits of information, they were able to keep the match alive in the press at least.

On June 20, 1923, three days before Pete left Big Bay, and five days after the second $100,000 payment was due Kearns/Dempsey, *The Mining Journal* carried yet another article that discussed the promoters’ difficulties with raising the necessary cash for the second payment; ticket sales weren’t going as planned. The fight’s promoters finally came up with the cash, though, with the help of additional bankers from Great Falls and other Montana towns. But Kearns, master of press manipulation either to gain additional free publicity or higher stakes, leaked that information. The national press corps, which had already arrived in Montana to cover the pre-match training of both fighters, duly reported it, and questioned whether Shelby would actually be able to come up with the remaining cash necessary to pull off the event.

Regardless, Pete stayed with his original plan to stop in Shelby during his cross-country trek to Alaska. Even if the promoters weren't able to pull off the match, the behind-the-scenes schemes and conniving would be worth Pete's time. So on the beautiful morning of July 2, Pete set out to find out what was happening with the match.

That same morning, all the Montana bankers who had intervened met with Jack Kearns in Great Falls, about an hour south of Shelby, where Dempsey was training for the fight. They tried to come up with the final $100,000-payment due Kearns/Dempsey that day, but could not. They said the press speculation on whether the match would take place greatly curtailed advance ticket sales. The outcome of that meeting was not announced outside the chamber building in Shelby until 3 a.m. on July 3.

The fight would proceed. But the business deal had changed— again. Since the promoters could not come up with the final installment due Kearns, they were forced to concede to his demands—to be put in charge of the gate, to take in all the cash paid for tickets at the stadium.

Pete, in the early morning hours of July 3, warily made his way back to his car, parked in the camp near the train depot, and wrote in his journal: "It seems the fight will go on."

Later that day, euphoria seemed to reign for all those who had so far traveled to Montana for the match. "Shelby cheered up last evening, after days of gloomy uncertainty, and began making the best of a rather bad case," wrote a correspondent for *New York American* on July 4, 1923. The two Wild West shows—a rodeo and stampede—paraded through Main Street. The cowboys and Blackfeet Indians dressed in their native costumes whooped and tried to lasso Shelby's two traffic cops. A Scottish Highlander bagpipe band that had crossed the border from Canada for the occasion piped up and down the street.

Pete watched the parade and attended a rodeo, which "was fine," he cryptically wrote in his journal. He then visited "a barn-like structure that served liquor and held bowery dances." He noted in his journal that at least "one-third of those attending wore overalls—everything goes here," before he retired in anticipation of the now on-again fight.

July 4, 1923, dawned with a brilliant blue sky—what the cowboys in Montana called a "high" sky. The temperature soared to near 100, but as most reporters noted at the time, the heat in Montana wasn't like that in the East; it was a "dry heat." By this time, Pete had acclimated to the temperatures—a heat wave had enveloped the Upper Peninsula of Michigan for the entire week prior to Pete's departure, with the mercury soaring into the mid-nineties, and the heat wave had continued throughout his entire trip—thus far.

The two Wild West shows staged another parade, leading into the arena around noon. The Elks Band and the Scottish Highlanders from Canada, plaid capes thrown over shoulders, took turns entertaining the assembling crowd inside the arena.

Official gate receipts were recorded at 7,966; those included Pete, who had paid the full price of $22 (advance tickets went for $50, $33, and $22). The seats in the inner circle, next to the ring, were fairly full, but as for the rest of the vast stadium "extending back were the 'great open spaces,' row upon row of pine boards, shining in their newness and pathetic in emptiness," wrote a reporter for *The Great Falls Tribune*.

Another crowd congregated outside the arena—mainly those who arrived by automobile or train that day. They refused to purchase tickets in case the fight did not go on as promised—Dempsey still had not arrived at the arena. One reporter said the hills outside the arena were "black" with Model T cars and people.

Kearns, Dempsey's shrewd manager who had bargained to take charge of the gate, decided there was only one way he could get the impatient crowd to come inside. He announced shortly before the fight was to occur that he would sell tickets at half price. The burgeoning crowd then rushed the arena. Kearns, reportedly, was stuffing silver in suitcases as quickly as he could.

Jack Dempsey then entered the ring at 3:30 p.m. Tall, muscular, and tanned from training outdoors, he was clad in white silk trunks with a red, white, and blue belt girding his waist with a blue sweater-coat over his shoulders. Five minutes later, Tommy Gibbons, the challenger, entered in a faded brown robe. The underdog, who had been made an honorary member of the Blackfeet Nation, was widely cheered, where Dempsey—deemed responsible for the failure of the match in terms of profit for the promoters—was jeered.

Some 100 newspapermen covered every aspect of the fight; it was also broadcast on radio—only the second time a fight was aired. And there were three "crow's nests" located atop the arena where movie men recorded the fight for a later show.

"They came to see a slaughter, to see the quick knockout of a man the New York State Boxing Commission once ruled was too small for the great Dempsey, a man thirty-four years of age, fighting a champion six years younger and fully twenty pounds heavier," reported the *New York American* (July 5, 1923). "Instead, they saw one of the greatest battles of recent years in the prize ring."

SHELBY'S ARENA: An overview of the 40,000 seat stadium that hosted the infamous World's Heavyweight Boxing Championship between Jack Dempsey and Tommy Gibbons on the Fourth of July in 1923. *Photo courtesy of Library of Congress.*

"Dempsey, the world heavyweight champion for four years and one of the most feared of his generation, won all but three or possibly four rounds from Gibbons. But he couldn't put the St. Paul challenger down for the count or even deck him. Gibbons, the crowd favorite all the way, fought a counter-punching and retreating battle," writes Otto Floto, who had witnessed every heavyweight title bout for the preceding thirty years, in the *Denver Post*.

"The actual fighting was all in one pattern—Dempsey stalking Gibbons across the ring, occasionally catching him and mauling him around, smashing his opponent with body punches," Floto continues.

"But Gibbons' elbows broke down the force of Dempsey's inside punches. He made the champion expend energy. Gibbons was always backing away from the hard blows, and at times he made the champion miss so badly that Dempsey looked annoyed," Floto writes. "Gibbons, however, was the first man up to that time who had stayed 15 rounds with Dempsey—for this reason alone the fight was considered a great battle."

Dempsey won by a decision, but he departed the arena and the train for Great Falls immediately after with blackened eyes.

He wasn't the only one hurt by the fight. Tommy Gibbons received nothing from the gate, although his training and housing expenses had been paid, and he gained some notoriety as well as a small amount of money from the producers for a movie of the fight.

But Shelby and its fight promoters were perhaps the most battered. Three banks in the area, which had put up huge sums of money to stage the fight, closed shortly after the gates closed. The First State Bank and the First National Bank in Shelby closed shortly after the fight, as well as the Stanton Bank in Great Falls.

"Kearns and Dempsey have been pointed out ever since as winners over three Montana banks," wrote John Lardner in the June 19, 1948, issue of *The New Yorker*. "This left Shelby with, for the time being, no banks at all and practically no assets. The oil boom subsided not long afterward. The arena was torn down and the lumber salvaged by the mortgage holders."

These businessmen squarely placed the blame for their losses on Kearns. It was his leaks to the press about their inability to come up with the cash installments on time, they said, that discouraged the majority of those planning to attend from traveling to Shelby.

"News got out, and the special trains were cancelled, and this in effect is what killed the Dempsey-Gibbons fight financially, even though the second payment was made, with the all-out help of [local banks] on June 16," writes Tony Dalich in the Summer 1965 issue of *Montana the Magazine of Western History*.

"Unfortunately, when the news that the fight definitely was to be held in the papers July 3, it was too late to reschedule canceled trains, too late for many fans to make the trip," Dalich writes.

DEMPSEY VS. GIBBONS: Dempsey lands a left and ends
up winning the 15-round match by a decision.
Photo courtesy of Library of Congress.

The only people who made money from the match were
Kearns and Dempsey, and possibly some of the concessionaires.
Kearns officially protested that they collected only $252,000 of the
promised $300,000. But he was seen, as he boarded the train to leave
Shelby, toting two canvas bags holding silver from the ticket sales
immediately before the fight. No one, apparently, counted the silver
Kearns collected. But in any case, what he made in those days was
a small fortune.

Pete made his way back to his camping spot near the train depot
that night.

It began to rain shortly after the match ended, turning the streets
into mud by morning. The motor tourists, including Pete, left in

droves. Pete left the park at 6 a.m. on July 5, heading toward Glacier Park and the West Coast beyond. Thinking about all he had witnessed and what lessons he could draw from this grand adventure kept him company, not just the blow-by-blow pummeling the two pugilists inflicted on one another, but the sideshows—the Wild West shows, the Blackfeet Indian Nation, the concessionaires, the newspapermen, and the movie people. Not to mention the behavior of the men who promoted the fight and what became of them.

Although he passed through some of the most scenic territory this country offers, Pete mentioned more, in his dry humor, about his car in the diary the next night than the gorgeous Glacier Park he drove through.

"July 6—got new timer a Milwaukee like old one. Engine is fine today. Climbs the Rockies like a goat. Drove the length of the park and there sure is some scenery. Fine lake full of trout but I did not fish. Paid 2.50 for timer, paid 2.50 park fee, gas .90, gas .70." And onward he drove.

Finally, after chasing twenty-one sunsets westward, Pete arrived in Seattle on Saturday, July 14, 1923. He immediately set out to find a boat that would ferry him and his Model T to Alaska. The Alaska Steamship Line quoted him the price of a ticket: $58.50 for himself and an additional $36.00 to ship the car. But the boat wouldn't load until the following Friday and sail until Saturday.

When Pete, dressed in his best suit, complete with vest and matching, ever-present fedora, showed up to have his car loaded on the steamship called *Alaska* the following Friday, he was handed a bill for $58.50 for himself, then one for $88 to ship the car. "We chewed a while, and I went up to see the head cheese, and he denied saying $36.00," Pete writes. "I went to the Pacific Steamship Line, and they said fare on an auto was $90, plus another $25 for me for a hotel stop in Valdez, so I paid the $88. Talk about Jesse

James; he was a gentleman," Pete goes on to say. Although he was extremely generous with his siblings, nieces, and nephews, Pete was exceedingly tight-fisted in his own business and personal affairs.

Pete suffered from seasickness during most of the voyage along the Inside Passage, but he managed several excursions out on the deck where he marveled at the mysteriously steamy and mountainous scenery his ship passed. He revived when he landed on solid ground. He sold his Model T in Valdez for $325, $15 more than he'd paid for it in Marquette, he said, and purchased a small piece of land with a cabin on Pennock Island, about three miles long and three-quarters of a mile wide and a mile off the coast of Ketchikan, Alaska.

KETCHIKAN: Here, an aerial view of the Tongass Narrows that shows Ketchikan with Pennock Island in the background. *Photo courtesy of Ketchikan Museums: Otto Schallerer image.*

Pete set out to meet with other fox farmers and learned all he could about the business. He also visited and examined many fishing operations, canneries, and small towns. He had a small, flat-bottomed wooden boat built, and he purchased an Elto outboard motor to ferry him between his island home and mainland Alaska.

Pete upgraded his 11' x 11' log cabin; he built a stove from an oil barrel to heat his cabin, made a bathtub from another oil barrel, and chinked the cracks between the logs with moss.

He cleared the land—he complained a little about the Muskeag, the swampy, moss- and underbrush-covered ground all about him. He built six pens and a corral to house four pairs of blue foxes he purchased for $300 per pair, which would be a little more than $5,000 per pair today.

ALASKA FOX FARM: Foxes eating in front of their pen on Blank Island, near where Pete settled in Alaska and purchased his blue foxes to bring back to Michigan.
Photo courtesy of Ketchikan Museums.

He speared a lot of salmon that he ate, shot some rabbits and ducks, and purchased a tremendous number of donuts in Ketchikan.

A short note in his diary for August 10, 1923, says: "Could not get mail. Post office closed on account of burial of president."

That is the only time Pete mentioned President Harding in his diary, although their journeys intersected at many points. Harding had left Washington on a private train on June 20, 1923. The trip was billed partially as an effort to improve trade with the Alaska Territory. But the trip—billed as The Voyage of Understanding— was also a bid to generate support for his re-election, especially in the wake of the Teapot Dome Scandal.

The president's entourage stopped at several cities along the way, where Harding gave impassioned speeches. He arrived in Tacoma, Washington, on July 5, and boarded the *USS Henderson* for his voyage to Alaska. The presidential party visited most of the hot spots in Alaska—many of the coastal cities Pete visited—as well as Mount McKinley National Park and the University of Alaska, and it even stayed at one inn where Pete stayed during his visits around the territory. Toward the end of his stay, the president began to exhibit symptoms of an illness, so his party sailed down the coast to San Francisco. President Harding died there on August 2, 1923.

Pete, however, stayed focused on his goals; at least that's what his journal indicates. His life that following winter revolved around learning to care for the foxes, tuning and repairing his Montgomery Ward radio, visiting with two fishermen who also lived on the island, and traveling to town for news, supplies, and mail.

It was an idyllic time for Pete—he obviously loved the outdoors, the isolated and quiet existence at his island home, and the challenge presented by his new "brood." On Sunday, November 25, 1923, Pete wrote that the foxes were "quite tame. One let me rough her head, leg, and chin at night. They eat good."

Pete named the one he regularly scratched Daisy, and called her mate Jack. They were clearly his favorites; he talked about them— and to them—daily. Cranky Jack, as Pete often referred to him, contracted some sort of illness, so Pete brought him into his cabin that night to care for him. The next day, Jack wasn't much better, so he brought him back out to the fox pen and dosed him with castor oil.

"He was so mad when I let him go he tried to bite me on the leg, then grabbed the feed pan and bit and shook it good, and then chased his mate around the pen and began to bark at me, but he got the caster oil," Pete writes. He was as determined to have his way as he was soft-spoken. When he said something, he meant it, even for his foxes.

But it seems those animals trusted him and listened to him, the way his siblings, nephews, and nieces did. Linda Bowers Bakken, now eighty-five, Pete's grandniece, remembers seeing him, an older man by this time, frequently sit on his front porch, fedora perched lopsided on his head to shade his light blue eyes.

"Squirrels would come up and sit on his knee for him to feed them for hours," Linda says. "He'd say, 'Linda if you want to come up here, you have to be very quiet.' I think I was a wiggly little thing," adds Linda. "But he was patient and coached me to be very still. And when I did sit still, the squirrels would come up to eat," she says.

But as kind and nurturing as he could be with people and animals, he was still—and utmost—in business to make money. Jack's condition worsened, and finally on December 13, 1923, Pete wrote: "Unlucky 13. Fox died six o'clock in morning. Gave him water every hour all night. Would not drink after three o'clock. Took his hide off, and it is fine. Very fat, heavy. It is much harder to skin a blue fox than a red one as they are so fat."

Even though Pete obviously loved those animals, and they were nearly all the company he had during that long winter on Pennock Island, he was practical to the point of hard-heartedness. He did what he had to do and accepted it for what it was—what he'd done his whole life.

ALL ABOARD: Pete, with his crated foxes, took a ferry from Ketchikan to Vancouver, then boarded this train to return to Marquette. *Family photo.*

It was that quiet determination—laced with a wry sense of humor—that got Pete through that long Alaska winter. In late September, Pete received a cable from J. B. Deutsch, who owned the lumber mill in Big Bay where Pete had been employed. Deutsch pressed Pete to return to Big Bay to run the mill for him, saying he would pay him an additional $3,000 per year if he agreed. But Pete stayed the course.

At the end of March in 1924, he built crates for his foxes and brought them back to Michigan—through Canada—on a train.

He indeed established his fox farm in Big Bay and did quite well. His niece, Mildred French Fleury, who grew up on the "same forty" as the fox farm, remembers Pete's fox farm, as well as the other two in Big Bay—one operated by the Tompkins family on the road to the Huron Mountain Club and the other by the Chaperon family on the dump road.

Millie says the younger members of the family played around the pens quite often. "He kept some females to breed, and there were always fox kits. I remember once when my cousin Betty was here from Grand Rapids, and we went over to play with the kits. She tried to hold one and it bit her under the chin," Millie says with a giggle. "I was kind of glad because she made fun of me because we were country hicks and they were city kids."

NIECES AND PUPS: Vernice French, left, and Betty Rhoades play with their uncle's blue fox pups on the farm in Big Bay during the summer of 1924. *Family photo.*

"I remember he sold lots of pelts and made good money," Millie adds. "We didn't watch, but they killed them and put the pelts on boards to stretch them out," Millie says. "And I remember all the old horses they bought to feed them—that's how my sister Vernice started riding horses. But we didn't watch them kill the horses either."

Then the stock market crashed in 1929, followed by the worst depression this country had seen. Pete eventually sold off all his foxes in the early 1930s.

It was another setback, but it didn't deter Pete, who had worked hard since the age of nine and remained actively engaged in business pursuits for the remainder of his life. It was during this period, from 1933 to 1945, that he became superintendent of maintenance at the Iron Mountain, Pequaming, L'Anse, and Big Bay mills for Henry Ford.

THE FOX PENS: Pete's foxes at his farm in Big Bay, where
he bred them to sell to other breeders or for
their pelts, quite valuable at the time. *Family photos*.

Agnes Swanson TenEyck, born in 1921, recalled that during the summer of her thirteenth year, her best friend, Alberta, whom the experimental town near L'Anse is named for, moved away from Big Bay. Her father, Fred G. Johnson, was superintendent over Ford's Upper Peninsula operations, and had been transferred to Iron Mountain. Several times in the summer of 1934, she and another friend who was also Pete's niece, Betty Raymen, commuted to Iron Mountain with Pete when he traveled there for work on Monday, and back again to Big Bay on Friday nights.

"He always had a new, black Ford, a very nice car, because he made good money," Agnes said. "And he was such a classy man. He always wore a suit and a black fedora in those days. He was quiet, didn't say too much because, well, if you knew Betty Raymen, she could talk. She and I chattered the whole three hours or so. I think he was glad to see us get out of that car!"

When Pete was home in Big Bay on weekends, he tinkered with his clothespin factory and fished. He loved to angle for brook trout, especially in the Yellow Dog River. But he always took time for the kids—the extended Raymen family now growing so that it was the grand nieces and nephews who tagged along after him.

Bert Bowers, eighty-eight, Pete's grandnephew, remembers that when he was about ten years old in 1943, he would walk up to our grandmother's house to visit with Pete. At the time, Pete was converting his clothespin factory from wooden to steel machinery. "Pete was an older and very ill man, but he would take the time to explain how all this machinery worked to me as if I were a grownup," Bert says. "I think he was trying to be a father figure to me too."

Every chance Pete got to sneak away, though, he'd drive the rugged ten miles or so "up on the Yellow Dog Plains" to get to his favorite fishing hole. In fact, Pete was alone in the woods, dropping a line in the Yellow Dog in August 1945, when he suffered a crippling heart attack. He managed to crawl up a steep bank to his car and drove himself to his sister's house in Big Bay. His family then transported him to St. Mary's Hospital, about thirty miles away in Marquette. He died there six days later at the age of sixty-seven.

Pete left the large tracts of land he'd accumulated and a little money to his siblings whom he had cared for all his life. He didn't leave behind a thriving business; he didn't patent parts or ideas or machinery that he'd cobbled together, nor become famous in any worldly sense. The only physical tributes to remain are a short street named for him, Raymen Street, and an unimposing headstone in the Big Bay cemetery. But this humble, unassuming man who lived a simple existence and always put his family first left an indelible legacy that endures to this day—one that continues to inspire members of his family and community. He lived a life of quiet determination, good deeds, unbounded curiosity, and continued pursuit of knowledge and adventure. Priceless values.

PETE'S PERCH: Whether to entertain his grand nieces and nephews, or to feed squirrels in his later years, Pete often sat on the back porch of his sister's house in Big Bay.
Family photo.

Acknowledgments

THE TELLING OF these stories would not have been possible without the help of my siblings: Bert, Linda, Allen, and Kay. But special thanks go to Bert—the oldest—with the longest, most vivid memory, not to mention he has great storytelling skills.

Several other family members contributed too. Among them, first cousins on my mother's side: Raymen P. (Tuffer) and Maxine Temple, Carol French Davis, Beverly Fleury Tobin, Julie Mitchell Mikulak, and Diane Raymen. Then, the cousins from my dad's side: Bill Bowers, Jerry Beerman, Sandy Beerman Sugarbaker, Shirley Temple Narovich, Arline Temple Erickson, Flora Nicholson Mena, and Lois, Bob, and Pat Burns.

Kay Burns Duncan was immensely helpful. She provided extensive material for the Burns family tree as well as photos. She also engaged with me on several telephone calls, answering exhaustive questions.

I can't possibly name every person I've interviewed, chatted with, or otherwise interacted with on behalf of these stories over the past couple of decades, especially those who are no longer with us. But I remember you all and will be indebted to you for your kindnesses for the rest of my life.

But there are many who deserve to be called out here:

Pete TenEyck helped me fact-check many, many entries. My sister Linda Bakken and nephew Philip Bakken read and provided feedback on early drafts.

Larry Chabot shared additional information that didn't make it in his book with me and answered lots of my questions.

Russell Magnaghi generously shared his time, knowledge, and expertise with me as well.

Michael Vaughn, Vice President of the Model T Club of America, provided detailed explanations of a 1923 Model T's working parts, especially the speedometer/tire mechanical interaction.

The research staffs at both the Ford Motor Company Archives and the Benson Ford Research Center cheerfully provided look-ups for what seemed like endless requests on my part.

Beth Gruber, research librarian at the Longyear Research Library in the Marquette Regional History Center, tirelessly helped me with innumerable research requests and additional information and photos.

I also greatly appreciate Betty A. Waring, who so presciently interviewed old-timers, including many of my family members, in the 1980s and published their memories.

Thanks also to Tyler Tichelaar for his invaluable editing and publishing skills. And to Larry Alexander for his deft hand at layout and publishing as well.

I've tried to be as careful and accurate as possible, and check and recheck documents. But if any mistakes do find their way in, the mistakes are mine alone. And I apologize.

Bibliography

Baraga, Frederic. *The Diary of Bishop Frederic Baraga.* Ed. Regis M. Walling and N. Daniel Rupp. Trans. Joseph Gregorich and Paul Prud'homme. Detroit, MI: Wayne State University Press, 2001.

Brooke, Lindsay. *Ford Model T: The Car That Put the World on Wheels.* Minneapolis, MN: Motorbooks, 2008.

Chabot, Larry. Saving Our Sons: How the Civilian Conservation Corps Rescued a Generation of Upper Michigan Men. Marquette, MI: North Harbor Publishing, 2009.

Isto, Sarah Crawford. The Fur Farms of Alaska: Two Centuries of History and a Forgotten Stampede. Fairbanks, AK: University of Alaska Press, 2012.

Kelly, Jason. Shelby's Folly: Jack Dempsey, Doc Kearns, and the Shakedown of a Montana Boomtown. United States: Jason Kelly, 2010.

Kohl, Johann Georg. *Kitchi-Gami: Life Among the Lake Superior Ojibway.* Trans. Lascelles Wraxall. St. Paul, MN: Minnesota Historical Society Press, 1985.

Longyear, John M. *Reminiscences.* Longyear Museum. Marquette Regional History Center, Marquette, MI. Unpublished Manuscript.

Magnaghi, Russell M. Prohibition in the Upper Peninsula: Booze & Bootleggers on the Border. Charleston, SC: American Palate, 2017.

Paddor, Scott, Dir. *The Big House.* "Alderson Federal Women's Prison." Narrated by Paul Sorvino. History Channel. Aired January 19, 1999. Available at YouTube. https://www.youtube.com/watch?v=aGwqOalGrls. Accessed September 23, 2022.

Roppel, Patricia. Land Mists: An Historical Guide to the Misty Fjords, Revillagigedo and Gravina Islands. Wrangell, AK: Patricia Roppel, 1998.

The Automobile Blue Book. Chicago and New York: Automobile Blue Book Pub. Co.. Volume 9, 1919. Volume 10, 1920. Volume 11, 1920.

Rydholm, C. Fred. *Superior Heartland: A Backwoods History.* Marquette, MI: C. Fred Rydholm, 1989.

Simonds, John O. CCC Big Bay: Recollections of Life in the Big Bay, Michigan, Camp of the Civilian Conservation Corps (1935-1936). N.p.: n.p., 2003. Copy located at Peter White Public Library, Marquette, MI.

SONGS for the CCC, Fort Brady CCC District, Compiled by Paul Olson, Educational Adviser, Camp Strongs. Published by The Northlander Headquarters, Fort Brady CCC District, Fort Brady, Sault Ste. Marie, Michigan.

Tichelaar, Tyler R. *Kawbawgam: The Chief, The Legend, The Man.* Marquette, MI: Marquette Fiction, 2020.

Underhill, John. "Camp Big Bay." NMU student paper prepared in 1985. Copy located at Northern Michigan University Archives.

Waring, Betty A. *The Story of Lake Independence: Big Bay, Michigan.* Marquette, MI: Northern Michigan University, 1984.

Waring, Betty A. *Yellow Dog Tales and Logging Trails to Big Bay, Michigan.* Marquette, MI: Lake Superior Press, 1986.

Waring, Betty A. Birch, Michigan: Gold'n Memories. Marquette, MI: Johnson's Printing Service, 1991.

About the Author

A NATIVE OF THE Upper Peninsula of Michigan, Faye Bowers received a BS in interdisciplinary studies (majoring in international relations and English) from Boston University.

Bowers spent the majority of her career reporting, writing, and editing for *The Christian Science Monitor*. She spent her last years there as a national security correspondent, mainly covering the US intelligence agencies and the Pentagon. Before that, she served as an editor in the international news department, and for a time as Deputy International Editor.

To ease into retirement, Bowers taught news writing and creative writing at Northern Michigan University for one year.

Since then, she has remodeled a couple of houses and worked on this collection of stories, some of which were previously published by the Michigan Historical Society.

Somewhat of a genealogy and history buff, Bowers is a member of the Massachusetts Society of Mayflower Descendants. She is proud of that heritage, as well as her Big Bay roots—going back to 1910.

9 798218 103125